TO THE USUAL SUSPECTS

TO THE USUAL SUSPECTS

One Word Questions

John Goldingay

paternoster press

First published in 1998 by Paternoster Press

04 03 02 01 00 99 98   7 6 5 4 3 2 1

Paternoster Press is an imprint of Paternoster Publishing,
P.O. Box 300, Carlisle, Cumbria, CA3 0QS, U.K.
http://www.paternoster-publishing.com

British Library Cataloguing in Publication Data
A catalogue record for this book is available from the British Library

ISBN 0-85364-927-8

Cover Design by Mainstream, Lanacaster
Typeset by WestKey Ltd., Falmouth Cornwall
Printed in Great Britain by
Caledonian International Book Manufacturing Ltd.,
Glasgow

Contents

1

Introduction

(i)

I laughed out loud over dinner (it is an odd thing about California, or our bit of it, that the post comes in the afternoon; I thought maybe it was because we were on the west coast and then realized that this ought to make the post come earlier). A letter from the publishers proposed turning the dedication of this book into its title. I laughed both because it was such a bizarre idea, and because it made sense – it wasn't just a catchy title. It was right. The usual suspects, the friends to whom I would have dedicated it, are more integral to it than a mere dedication implies. They are the people who have often kept my wife Ann and me going over recent years, indeed have often enabled us to thrive and not merely survive. They are the wheelchair-pushers I describe in chapter 9.

Over the past decade nothing has been more influential in shaping who I am, what I do, what I say, and what I write than my wife Ann and the coping with her multiple sclerosis and increasing disability that we have to do together (and sometimes apart). Everything I write is in some sense hers too, even the abstruse academic things, because I would be a different person were I not married to her. The fact that I would be much more of a so-and-so if I had not had to live through the last ten years with Ann does not make her illness any easier to accept. In some ways it makes it grimmer: why should I get a bit less immature at her expense? But in other ways it takes the edge off the grimness.

Once Ann herself hoped to write something about her experience of illness, but the very progress of the illness has made that impossible. I have often thought that one day I might write something about it, and I suddenly realized that this is the moment and this is the book. At least in part it is because we are at a moment of transition in our lives. After twenty-seven years at St John's College, Nottingham, I wrote what follows as we were preparing to move to Pasadena for me to take up a teaching post there. It means that the suspects cannot be part of our lives as they have been. If you cannot work out whether we are in the UK or the USA, this is because we are on an aeroplane.

That is a joke. One or two of my students in California have expressed some confusion about not being able to tell when I am joking, because I joke with a straight face. Come to think of it, some of my students in Nottingham had the same problem. In reality, I wrote a first draft of this book in the last weeks in Nottingham, and the final version in the first weeks in California.

The book looks at some basic questions about being Christian and being human which I have tried to think about for one reason or another over recent years. Because they are basic questions, I wanted to give the chapters one-word titles (well, it made sense to me). I planned to call the book *One Word Questions*, to draw attention to the fact that the very nature of these questions often precludes their having one-word answers (that made sense to me, too). To signal that they were (slightly) postmodern-style soundings rather than a systematic presentation of an organized whole, I decided to arrange them in alphabetical order (yes, that too).

Ann stands within the frame of all the chapters that follow, sometimes visibly, sometimes invisibly. She drives me back all the time to basic questions about what it means to be human with God. When it is some other context that presses a question, she provides key elements in the subconscious framework within which I think about it. In important ways I fail her, but at least here I acknowledge her.

Admittedly all that deserves footnoting with a health warning. None of us understand ourselves, and usually anything we say about ourselves has to be taken with a block of salt. It is always wise to assume that there is a lot more iceberg below the surface which we cannot see than there is above the surface which we can see (as Freud said, I suppose). Further, when people give you the impression that they are being amazingly open about themselves, it is a wise assumption that there are lots of other things that they are being careful to conceal. There is lots of invisible iceberg that they are well aware of and intend to keep concealed, at least for the moment. I know that is true of me. But I will tell you most of what I know.

I named a number of the suspects in the dedication of *After Eating the Apricot*, but by the time the book came out, there were already others who deserved to have been included. So this time I decided to let them be anonymous. They know who they are. This is Ann's book, but it is also theirs. Only the names have been hidden, and the sex sometimes changed, to protect the innocent.

If you are not a film buff, you may appreciate my explaining that 'the usual suspects' is an ironic and slightly affectionate phrase from the Humphrey Bogart/Ingrid Bergman film *Casablanca*, released the year after I was born, to which the 1995 film *The Usual Suspects* has recently paid homage. There the phrase is very ironic, here also very affectionate. I have just discovered that David Thomson in *A Biographical Dictionary of Film* calls *Casablanca* 'a women's picture for men', a further irony as the publishers regarded *After Eating the Apricot* as a man's book for women. Thomson also sees *Casablanca* as embodying 'bittersweet romanticism' (one or two of the suspects will smile at that), 'the sort of unblinking tosh, set deep in never-never land, that is the essence of Hollywood'. That must be why it has been shown twice in three months on our local 'public service' TV channel (the nearest American equivalent to the BBC, but they have to keep appealing to you for money). I watched it both times. And Thomson sees Bogart as playing himself (in *High Sierra*) when he is being 'the lonely, self-sufficient, middle-aged man, aware of the fate that awaits him'. Well, *Casablanca* has its tosh moments, but I think the fact that it is handling a real human dilemma (the relationship between love and responsibility/commitments) is reflected in the fact that its theme keeps recurring in films (*Brief Encounter*, *Falling in Love*, *The Bridges of Madison County* . . .).

(ii)

Ann and I met over a boiled egg (well, two) at a Christian students' conference in April 1963. The boiled eggs were soft on the outside and hard on the inside; I have always wondered how they did that. I was wearing my name badge upside-down as a way of drawing attention to myself and to my uncooperative instincts. I succeeded, but Ann and I were both involved with other people at the time. Each of us returned to the next year's conference looking for the other.

I had a bad conscience with regard to that previous romance (indeed I still have) but at least I could claim that I was now uninvolved. Ann could not, which gave her an anxious train journey a few weeks later as she travelled back from Stockton-on-Tees where her parents lived to London where she was a medical student. There might have been two young men waiting for her at King's Cross. I was the only one who turned up, so I won. Next term I took my final exams for my theology degree; she sent me a red rose each day that week.

Another April day two years later I went to spend a day with her on the eve of my last term at theological college before I was ordained. It was a warm Sunday evening as we left her flat in Hampstead with some friends to walk to the underground to get to evening church. As she crossed the road, she was limping. Good medical student that she was, she had made the most alarming diagnosis possible, though she was not histrionic about it. She believed she had disseminated sclerosis, as it was then called. Multiple sclerosis in due course became the normal term as the disease itself became better known. It involves (I expect she told me) a malfunctioning of the nervous system which can affect different parts of the body and result in those parts not responding to messages from the brain because of demyelinizing of the sheathes on the nerves which carry the messages. Next day she walked into her hospital and reported her symptoms and diagnosis. She was treated with due scepticism but by the end of the week was proved right. The next Sunday I hitch-hiked to London on another lovely sunny spring day to see her in hospital. I felt a strange joy and was not at all surprised to get a lift in a sports convertible on the edge of Bristol which took me the hundred miles to London in one go. The medics had started Ann on a course of a cortisone drug whose initials are ACTH and which has something to do with pig's bladders. This did the trick (how they discovered it would do so I have never known). After a few weeks she was walking normally.

The strange joy came to be associated with three passages from scripture. One was brought to our attention by Alec Motyer, Ann's vicar and before that my inspiration, mentor and role model as Old Testament theologian. He would want to disown some of my thinking now, but he still loves us. He must have gone to see Ann in hospital and then written to me, and he included an allusion to a passage of scripture which he happened to have been reading that day. It was the story of the wedding at Cana in Galilee, where one of the guests comments, 'You have kept the good wine till last.' God does that, Alec commented. It has been an important promise, though not one yet fulfilled except in paradoxical ways.

The other two passages were variations on another point. I wrote them on the flyleaf of a book of Alec's expositions of Philippians, *The Richness of Christ*, which I gave to Ann; they made we weep the other day when I was packing this book among others and spotted the inscription/dedication, along with some more personal words to the woman I loved. One of the passages was a phrase from that letter to the Philippians, 'for me to live is Christ' (1.21). The other was some words from Psalm 73, which tells of someone's agonizing about the tough side to life which had nevertheless led to the realization:

I am always with you;
you hold me by my right hand.
You guide me with your counsel,
and afterwards you will take me into glory.
Whom have I in heaven but you?
And earth has nothing I desire besides you.
My flesh and my heart may fail,
but God is the strength of my heart
and my portion for ever.

Both summoned each of us to make God the one person who counted, so that the other human being whom we loved did not become an idol. It was much easier to mean those words then than it has been to mean them during some of the subsequent years.

The following April Ann had a relapse of the multiple sclerosis, this time affecting her eyes, but again the ACTH did the trick. At the time we were 'unoffically engaged'. I am not sure whether this category of relationship still exists. It meant we knew that we were committed to marrying each other, and we believed that this was God's will, and our commitment was a semi-public fact, but Ann was not wearing a ring. The reason was that her parents disapproved of me. This was partly because of some aspects of my character (I was not respectful enough or formal enough), but partly because they were very fond of their only daughter and were sad at the prospect of losing her.

During this spell in hospital, a staff nurse told Ann that she had no right to get married with an illness like hers, and certainly had no right to become a mother. The words still haunt Ann and make her wonder whether she did the right thing.

In a sense questions like that are pointless, of course. A few years ago, before appraisal as such was invented, we had on the college staff a peer review and support system which we called 'triads', despite the word's connotations of Chinese mafia. Once a year each of us would review the previous year and discuss work and personal issues with two other people. One year things with Ann had evidently been tough and we had discussed this and talked about how I coped, and the then principal's notes of the discussion said something about my nevertheless affirming that I was still glad that I had married her. That did not seem quite right. I do not mean that I was not glad, but that this was somehow not the framework for thinking about the matter. When you discover that the person you have fallen in love with has an illness such as multiple sclerosis, you cannot then have a solemn discussion about whether you are glad you fell for this person or whether you should decide to terminate the love relationship. At least, I could not do that. To ask the question is to deny the reality of what has already happened. It is to deny yourself.

As it happened my tutor when I was at college had a wife with a chronic illness, and I remember a Friday afternoon that summer I learned of Ann's illness when he also went as near as he could to inviting me to reconsider whether I wanted to take on what I might be taking on. I think I somehow knew that I would only understand what he meant when I was thirty years older, the way you only understand your own parents when you are a parent of teenagers and adults yourself, and I knew that then it would be too late, or rather that it was already too late, and that he knew it was too late, but that he still had to say it. And I am glad that he did, not because it was any use to me then, but because it is somehow of use to me now to know that he knew how it would be for me and knew the pain of it but knew that I could not get out of it (and I wish I had found a way of telling him this before he died). Because relationships lay necessities upon you. You cannot go back on the commitment of love without betraying yourself as well as the other person.

I do not know whether that staff nurse did well to say the equivalent words to Ann, those words that still haunt her. When Ann recalls them to me as she does from time to time, one thing I say back is that if she had not married and become a mother, our sons Steven and Mark would not have existed. They might be prepared to view that as a shame, as might their own lady-loves. I was reminded of this when Ann and I went on a rehabilitation centre outing to see the film *One Fine Day*, in which one divorced parent is asked by her son whether she still loves his father and she replies, 'I will always love him because he gave me you.' (Well, OK, I know it's cheap, but I don't care.)

Ann and I always say how grateful we are to God that Ann was so well all through Steven and Mark's childhood, but I know they were aware of Mommy having this illness, and that they paid a cost in some sense. One year when Mark was seven or eight, Ann had a spell in hospital and her mother was staying with us. She made a remark about 'when Mommy is better'. Mark said quietly, 'Mommy will never be really better.' A little while later, when Steven was in his early teens, I was taking him to see Ann on the occasion of a subsequent spell in hospital. As I drove and he sat in the back seat, I asked whether he worried about her, and he said, 'Well, yes, I do really.' I did not know where to go with the conversation from there, though I now realize that there is some kind of inner link between that moment and an occasion more than a decade later when Ann had had the seizure I refer to in a moment and Steven and I stood outside the University Hospital in Nottingham and wept on each other's shoulders.

Yes, they have paid a cost. But I also tell Ann that whatever cost there might have been to them in their mother's having this illness, it is more than counterbalanced by the potential positive shaping that it will have effected upon them, the sense in which it has contributed to the making of them as human beings, as it continues to do in the shaping of me.

We eventually married six months after that second spell in hospital during which the staff nurse issued her rebuke. Within weeks Ann was unplanned-ly pregnant. She was on the pill, which was a novelty in the 1960s, and was allegedly the innovation that was taking all the worry and hazard out of sex. The day after a visit to the hospital which established that Ann was indeed pregnant, the *British Medical Journal* carried a report of some research which suggested that the particular pill Ann was taking was not as 'safe' as some others. We were already in a position to confirm that.

Ann's parents were livid with me. It could not have been worse if we had been unmarried. They had always been looking forward to their daughter qualifying as a doctor and coming back home to practise, and I had imperilled that, first by marrying her and then by getting her in the family way. But there was a more serious problem. Pregnancy and giving birth are big strains on a person (nothing to parenthood, I am tempted to add, but that is probably a male perspective). Stress is a major factor in precipitating relapses of multiple sclerosis. Ann's neurologist (one of her own lecturers for whom she had great respect) took the view that Ann had no business having a baby within months of a second attack in a year, and recommended she have an abortion. It was the end of 1967, the year of the passing of the Abortion Act.

We thought and talked and prayed, as you would, and eventually asked for a second opinion. We went to see another neurologist, who declined to demur from his colleague's recommendation but was a model in the way he put the facts before us in order to help us make our own decision. The decisive comment for me (though Ann does not remember this bit) was that it was clear from Ann's notes that she had had two attacks of the illness, but that from examining her he could find no trace of their effects. He could not remember seeing someone who had had two attacks of the kind that Ann evidently had had, and who was now as well as she was. I did not infer that she had been 'healed' in the sense that she no longer had the illness, but it was enough as a sign that we were to trust God for the future.

The pregnancy proceeded uneventfully, as far as the multiple sclerosis was concerned. Ann had high blood pressure and was in hospital for some weeks to keep that under control, but this can happen with any pregnancy. One Monday at 3.00 a.m. the hospital rang to tell me I had better come now if I wanted to see the action. I remember sitting at traffic lights on the Holloway Road in North London wondering whether it was really necessary for them to take so long to change at 3.30 in the morning (I recall being tempted to ignore them, but I cannot remember whether I did). In those days it was not customary for husbands to be present at births, but as a medical student Ann had pulled strings. I had always said I did not really believe what one was told about how babies were born because it seemed implausible. Ann was more concerned for me to see with my own eyes and then shut up than to have me holding her hand. By 7.45 I was convinced, and back at Morning Prayer in church in Finchley.

Actually I have a more vivid memory of bringing Ann home from hospital a few days later. Steven had quite long fingernails at birth and was inclined to scratch himself, so on the way home we had to stop near the same traffic lights to buy him some mittens. So Ann went into the baby clothes shop *and left me on my own, with the baby on the back seat.* What would I do if he woke up? They were the most anxious five minutes of my life, more real in memory than the actual birth is.

As Steven has grown to be taller than me and to go to university in the city where I was brought up and to teach me how to use a computer, and has become a systems analyst, and especially as I married him to Sue last year, I have often reflected on the fact that he was supposed to have been flushed down the toilet. I have also come to realize that Steven's being born then, and Mark three years later, contributed significantly to the healing of relationships with Ann's parents. Ann's father died when Mark was a baby, but at least that meant that he had seen and held his two grandsons, and played with one. If they had been born in accordance with *our* plan, I doubt whether that would have been so; and Ann thus comments that God's family planning turned out to be wise.

Ann's mother lived for another fifteen years, and I realized near the end how much she and I loved each other. She was a gifted and enthusiastic knitter, and the symbol of her love was making me sweaters, the last of which I wore for her funeral to honour her (this also gave me the excuse not to wear a suit). In those last years it was difficult to believe that we had once so resented each other. All the resentment had melted away so that it could now only be recalled as something that had happened on another planet. And the thing which had melted it away was our having in common as a fierce and frightful bond the fact that the person we both most loved had this terrible illness. This, too, does not make the illness seem all right, but I have to acknowledge that is the kind of fruit that the illness has had, and continues to have.

Over the twenty years which followed those first two attacks, from time to time Ann would have relapses of the illness, but the medics were able to control it. So over that period she was lady vice-president of the London University Christian Union (there was a stained-glass ceiling at that point in those days, if not now), qualified as a doctor, had two children, brought them up, worked in General Practice and in Family Planning(!), and completed postgraduate training in psychiatry to the point of gaining Membership of the Royal College of Psychiatrists. In recent years I have had to become more of a 'new man', but I was not much of one in the 1970s. Only when it became necessary did I learn to cook. Only from my sons – whom Ann got a grip of – did I learn to use the washing machine. Only this year did I finally find the instructions for the steam iron and try them out. Well, I was afraid of those brown marks that men with irons end up with in comedies. That is my story.

A particular concrete memory still amuses me. One May, Ann had another relapse of the illness, at a time when our doctor was on holiday. The doctor who came to see Ann decided to try a different form of the ACTH, which sent Ann batty. More specifically she became manic-depressive – for instance, trying to do more things than it was possible to do. One effect was that she would wake at dawn (pretty early at that time of year I remember, wearily) with a word from the Lord. Ann was not usually a word-from-the-Lord Christian, but such religious delusions were understandable enough on the part of a religiously inclined person. Except that when she went on to read the Scripture Union portion for the day, which happened to come from the Psalms, and to read Derek Kidner's comments on it, each day her word from the Lord would reappear somewhere there . . . I still do not know what to make of that, except to put it in my scrapbook of things that happen because God thinks they are good fun.

With hindsight, I realize that the pattern of the illness was changing as Ann finished her psychiatric training. She then began further training in psychotherapy, and things started to fall apart. For a variety of reasons, or in a variety of ways, the job and the training did not work. We thought it was partly because her supervisor was not a Christian and was concerned that she might bring God into her work. I thought it might be that she was simply not good at it. I suspect now that the illness was beginning to take away the degree of concentration and insight that this very demanding speciality requires. But that did not occur to me for years. How it felt to me at the time was that she simply lost interest in *me*. She would come home each day and need simply to debrief on how grim the day at work had been. I came to feel that she had left me. I was simply someone to talk to (or at) as soon as the boys had finished their meal. Each evening we would sit at the table alone as I received this blow-by-blow account of whatever it had been and of the worries it entailed. There was never a question about how I was or what was happening to me.

At least that is how I remember it. I feel a bit pathetic about it now, but I know it felt real at the time. I remember how I would wake up in the night and be unable to get back to sleep and would go downstairs and sit on the settee and cry out to God in the manner of the Psalms, feeling alone.

Nowadays our students know I enthuse about the Psalms and about the freedom in pain and in joy that they give us, and many of them come to share something of that. It was new to me then. Once when I was an assistant minister back in the 1960s we were discussing a change in the form of services. I commented in the church council that I thought this would be good because it would involve less singing of the Psalms. My vicar withered me with a look across the vicarage lounge (he was practised at that, but I was fairly impervious) and said, 'My boy, one day you will need the Psalms.' The moment had come.

For Ann it was the beginning of a period of years which seem to have been unqualified loss. Instead of having occasional relapses she began a gradual continuing process of declining in mobility, self-sufficiency, and other capacities. She needed a stick to walk with, then she could not drive, then she needed a wheelchair. She would forget things, so it was no longer safe for her to work at all. Her retirement through ill-health became effective on the day I became a theological college principal. In one sense that seems a cruel coincidence, though in another it points to the way she then began a ministry. It was a different ministry from the one some people imagined she might undertake, one which involved counselling or teaching people counselling. It was the inactive but powerful ministry of a person who had once been able to do all that, and now cannot.

Over the years Ann has been ministered to and prayed with by many of the high-profile figures in the healing circuit, but it seems that whatever is God's intention for and through Ann is to be achieved by not healing her of her illness rather than by doing so. The year after she gained her MRCPsych we had a visit from a John Wimber 'Signs and Wonders' team in Derby. I went partly because I wanted to look open-minded. In the course of working through the standard teaching material for such events, the leader told us about his handicapped daughter who had *not* been healed, and about how God used her to minister to people, not merely despite her disability but through it. This was not my image of the 'Signs and Wonders' enterprise, and I immediately knew that this was a man with whom I could do dealings. He lived in the real world, in the way that I have to. I wanted to believe that God healed and to pray for people's healing, but I needed also to be able to handle it when God did not heal – not merely to handle it but to make sense of it and perhaps see the other forms of healing in it.

As I write, Ann has just come home after spending a short time in a rehabilitation centre. She can just about feed herself, but she cannot stand up. She loves the birds and the squirrels in our garden, always comments on the sound of police cars and aircraft passing, and enjoys television programmes such as *Ready, Steady, Cook*. She loves people and has an extraordinary capacity to arouse love in them.

An incident sums it up for me. We went to some student friends for dinner. At the end of the meal, Ann was enthusing over the cheesecake for which she had had no room (having partaken of the alternative dessert). Our host offered to put some in a doggy bag, and did so. Then after tea Ann asked her whether she had any chocolate to go with our coffee. She did not have any, but thought for a moment or two and then set off on foot to buy a (large) block from a petrol station. It was somehow an expression of a deep love and acceptance of Ann as she is in her childlikeness, of the kind that I hope I show something of. And on Ann's part I wonder whether in her lack of inhibition she is behaving the normal human way and letting us behave the normal human way. It is, after all, normal to love to know something that another person whom we care about really wants, because we can then get a kick out of giving it. But we hesitate to reveal the little things that we really want, and so deprive the other person of the thrill of fulfilling this desire. This sounds horribly pious, but what I sometimes find myself thinking is that it is a privilege to look after someone, to serve someone.

Yes, I do get annoyed with Ann, particularly if her discomfort or tiredness is expressed as apparent annoyance with me. But most of the time she is capable of smiling with as much happiness in her eyes as I ever remember. Even though she grieves over her loss of independence and her inability to work, she lives life moment by moment, often enjoying the surprises of someone who does not remember what was supposed to happen next.

(iii)

Perhaps I ought to tell you the outline of my story, too. Here is how I once expressed it for a theological students' journal. There are overlaps with some of the above and things that may make little sense if you are a not a theologian, but I thought it was best to leave it approximately as it was, except for adding a closing entry in the same style as the others.

Aged 0: chosen, called to be a theologian, born, baptized.

Aged 12: decide to learn Greek instead of German in the hope that it will improve my awful Latin (in those days you needed Latin to get into Oxbridge, and my school did not recognize the existence of other universities). This has more eventual influence on me as a theologian than the fact that as a choirboy I listen to the sermons of a curate called David Jenkins. Moral: God uses even the pre-Christian decisions you take.

Aged 13: converted. Start sharing my minister's enthusiasm for reading the New Testament in Greek. Yes, I too think this is disgustingly precocious. Eventually do A-level Religious Education as well as Greek, Latin, and Ancient History. Puzzle school chaplain by insisting on a sixth-century date of Daniel and on 'propitiation' not 'expiation' etc. in an essay on Romans – but win a prize for the essay, my long-precious *Young's Concordance*.

Aged 18: enthuse over Helen Shapiro's records. Discover it is easy to get into Oxford if you want to study theology. Take Hebrew because I have already done Greek. Start with Old Testament and never get beyond that because of the inspiration of John Baker (later Bishop of Salisbury) as tutor and Alec Motyer as preacher; expect to move on to New Testament, Doctrine, Church History, etc., in heaven. Fortunate to be studying when it is respectable to reckon that Abraham existed, but decide I do not after all find three Isaiahs and a second-century Daniel incompatible with scriptural authority/inspiration. Regarded by Christian Union as dangerous combination of Christian and enthusiast for theology. Meet wife-to-be at UCCF conference; take her to Beatles concert at Hammersmith Odeon.

Aged 24: ordained. Read von Rad and John Owen as curate. Campaign for abolition of Psalms from services; vicar prophetically declares, 'Young man, you will need the Psalms one day.' Write paper to show that Anglican order of ministry is scriptural. Ponder/agonize over theological issues raised by nascent charismatic movement with aid of J. B. Phillips's *The Young Church in Action*. Get offered theological college teaching posts and think maybe someone is trying to tell me something. Do MTh course at King's, London, and fail; friends kindly think this must be problem with King's, not me. Publish dissertation in *Tyndale Bulletin*, along with other work from MTh study – including in due course *Songs From a Strange Land* (based on college Bible expositions).

Aged 28: join St John's, Nottingham, staff and stay a long time. Borrow Eric Clapton's *Layla* from Graham Cray and pronounce it world's greatest record. Discover the word 'hermeneutics' and write paper on the subject, also paper in the *Churchman* on how one can hold together a belief in inspiration and an acceptance of critical approaches to scripture. Acceptance of charismatic theology gradually becomes experience as well as theory; it helps me understand how inspiration worked. Acknowledge that there is no scriptural theology of ordination, but you cannot expect to agree with everything in a church, can you? Realize that the Old Testament is my idol and repent. Speak at Greenbelt; astonished and excited to discover that Christian rock music could be worth listening to.

Aged 31: spend summer in Israel, climb Mount Sinai (if that was it), narrowly missing Egyptian army attempt to recapture Sinai. Find Israel wondrously informing of my appreciation of scripture and the having-happened-ness of the gospel. Henceforth try to get back there as often as possible, often taking student groups and enjoying watching their similar (or different) reactions.

Aged 33: principal suggests I really should do a PhD, which leads to *Approaches to Old Testament Interpretation* and *Theological Diversity and the Authority of the Old Testament*. Reviewers reckon either that I am too willing to concede ground to critical theories or that I believe too much in the Old Testament as divine revelation, so I conclude I am on right lines. Meet Brevard Childs. Apply unsuccessfully for university jobs; come to realize that a believing, worshipping, preaching community is a good context in which to study critical theology, for me as for students, because it helps me keep theology in relationship with God and other aspects of real life. So when later I get asked to consider university posts, I say 'No'.

Aged 35: asked to contribute to the Word Commentary series, but reckon I cannot take on other commitments. They respond by sending me contract for Daniel – I suspect on the strength of a three-page article in *Themelios*. I am intrigued, try to be open-minded about a sixth-century date but conclude that the critics are right, though am more interested in expounding the book's theological significance.

Aged 41: my wife Ann's long-standing multiple sclerosis starts to become much more troublesome. This leads me into a much deeper involvement with the Psalms, new discoveries about the nature of prayer, new proving of scripture's word-of-God-ness in its manifold capacity to speak to me in my pain, and into editing *Signs, Wonders, and Healing*. Live not least by a word from God given to me through Tom Smail: 'I will make the north wind your warmth, the snow your purity, the frost your brightness, and the night sky of winter your illumination.' Meet Walter Brueggemann. First perform with a semi-professional rock band; write 'Born in a UPA'. Learn from my son how to word-process, though live by the principle 'You don't read incomprehensible manuals, you hit keys until the computer does what you want. You experiment until you have learned how it works.' Buy second-hand set of Barth's *Dogmatics*. Discover Van Morrison. Discover France.

Aged 45: made Principal of St John's, rather unexpectedly because we were not due to need another one for a while. Cultivate habits such as wearing odd socks to put people off from thinking of other distracting appointments for me, but stop cutting my own hair and buy dog-collar. Encouraged by a word from God given through Barry Kissell: 'You had a vision for the college, and you had begun to think that it would never come true, but it will come true.' Encourage development of courses which take theology more seriously (Honours BTh, Graduate BTh, MA, MPhil/PhD). Form own band ('Two priests, three ordinands, and a pregnant woman'). *Young's Concordance* displaced by Analytical RSV equivalent.

Aged 49: finish expansion of hermeneutics paper into a large book (two, it turned out). Conclude that Origen is a better guide than Warfield to the implications of inspiration (inspiration means the details of the text are designed to say something to us, it does not merely mean that they are minutely factual). Begin work on Isaiah

40–66 for International Critical Commentary. Promise to write an Old Testament theology before I die. Discover I share birthday with Errol Flynn. Find myself involved (by accident really) in controversy over interfaith worship. Discover Helen Shapiro has been converted. Reflect on the fact that I subconsciously assumed when I was twenty or so that once you were adult nothing else ever happened; actually God never stops doing new things with you (at least, not so far). 'Old men should be explorers' (T. S. Eliot). 'I shan't retire – the habit of writing is too powerful' (V. S. Pritchett). 'When you're over the hill you pick up speed' (anon). Squeezed out of own band by over-gifted students.

Am blessed with a college tradition of sharing management among staff (I ran the college before being principal, really) and with an assistant who has a vast enthusiasm for administration, so I can still both teach and research (wouldn't have had the job otherwise). Take seriously the observation that 'Jobs in the Church of England are almost entirely what the incumbent makes of them. To make anything of them, he must first get on top of the administration.' Also the observation of an England cricket captain, 'My general principle is to create a buoyant atmosphere in which we can all be relaxed, and thus deliver the goods more effectively.'

Age 54: join Ronnie Scott's jazz club. Publish *After Eating the Apricot*, whose title at least has people guessing. Buy suit (from charity shop) for son's wedding. Discover that I am ENTJ (Myers-Briggs) and that failure is my Enneagram starting point, but do not manage to resolve controversy over whether or not in Colour-Me-Beautiful I am spring, upon which opinions differ. Resign as Principal of St John's College. Visit California and get appointed Old Testament Professor at Fuller Seminary in Pasadena.

(iv)

The story goes that the one-time manager of Liverpool Football Club, Bill Shankley, said of football that it was not a matter of life and death; it was more important than that. I feel the same about music. And music therefore interrelates with my life with God, especially the music which articulates the kind of tough questions we are concerned with in this book. So in some of the chapters that follow I am including references to rock records which help me think about these questions. This is rock as it feeds or expresses my relationship with God, whether or not it may reflect/reveal the composers'/performers' relationship with God.

Defining 'rock music' is notoriously difficult. I suppose I am using the term to denote music which, compared with most 'pop music', may be louder and/or more serious lyrically and/or more demanding musically and/or more adult-oriented. Admittedly one of my colleagues mutters about people who continue to listen to the kind of music that other people stopped listening to when they grew up (I recently realized that giving up childish things when he became a man was one of Paul's chief problems). But little of the material that I refer to is esoteric. I know it through Radio 1, television, the newspapers, or the rock magazine *Q*.

I did once write a punk song myself (and one rap and one post-feminist blues). The first time I visited the Nine O'Clock Service, in its fairly early days at St Thomas's, Crookes, I was overwhelmed by the way it brought together two parts of my life. I had never before felt so keenly the scandal of their separateness. The music was not exactly my kind of music, but it was much closer to it than the usual *Songs of Fellowship* allegedly-modern fare. It made my foot thump in a way that worship songs do not. And I felt a grief which abides after nearly a decade that worship cannot involve my whole person in the manner of a gig at Rock City in Nottingham or at Ronnie Scott's.

Graham Kendrick is wonderful but it isn't rock and roll –
I want music with guts as well as music to bless my soul.
They say that all the types of music were sacred song at the start;
Blues and soul and rock and roll have praise and prayer at the heart.
So why don't songs for worship reflect the whole of the art?

Graham Kendrick is wonderful but it isn't like the blues –
It can't directly express it when you're hurt and when you lose.
I've stood and waved and clapped and cried and cheered at the NEC,
I'm now the sole survivor of the chaplains of Rock City,
And I wish when I came to worship it moved the whole of me.

Graham Kendrick is wonderful but it doesn't thump like rock –
It doesn't assault your eardrums or leave you in a state of shock.
I've no objection to tambourines and I like the sound of a flute,
But I also like to be driven to stamp up and down with my boot.
Is it really impossible for rock songs to be the Spirit's fruit?

Graham Kendrick is wonderful but what about r and r?
I want to put rhythm and blues together with hosanna and hallelujah.
There are theological reasons as you'd expect from the way that I've
    trod.
In the end there is only one music because there is only one God.
In the end there is only one music because there is only one God.
In the end there is only one music 'cos in the end there is only one
    God.

(v)

As you look back, you sometimes see patterns in things that
seemed unrelated at the time. One year we had an unhappy term
in the college. It seemed to be in some sense my fault as principal
for not getting on top of the problem before it felt like a major
crisis, and I ended the year convinced that it was time I left, for
the college's sake and for mine. By the autumn it was looking as
if it was right to stay, but I was not feeling that I had recovered
from the battering of that preceding year. I imagined the next
three terms could only be downhill all the way, because that had
usually been the pattern – we spent thirty-odd weeks each year
giving out and absorbing problems, and then God restored us over
the summer if we were lucky. I say 'had usually been the pattern'
because that negative patterning did change, and I believe that

Ann's influence on college was somehow one of the reasons for this.

I remember a colleague praying with me one day that autumn. I was confessing to the fear that although I now knew that this was still the right place to be, I did not think I had the strength to sustain the year. I was not sure I could hack it. She prayed that the restoring that had been going on would continue abundantly. I remember thinking 'fat chance of that', the way you do when someone prays daft things for you. But there is a verse in James about the prayer of a powerful woman being righteous in its effects, and over the autumn and winter I could feel my strength continuing to build up. Which was as well, because there was a lot to think through and handle in college that year.

After the first session of our course in Spirituality that term, I sat in chapel for a few minutes, not sure why I was doing so, and a student came over and hugged me, and to my surprise I burst into tears. As I have hinted already, for better or for worse I am radically insensitive about emotions in public, but on this occasion it was partly because of who it was. I knew about a particular sadness in his life which meant that his experience and mine with Ann gave us something in common. Yet those particular tears seemed to be more about the demands on me than about the pain inside me. I expressed it in terms of having more balls to keep in the air than I had juggled before, and the problem was not whether I could actually keep them in the air, but whether I believed that I could do so.

When it came to the next term, there was a particular week which I knew would be especially busy. It was the first week of the new semester and the beginning of my busiest teaching half-term of the year, with two revised courses to start and a new one to launch. My student group was beginning its period of responsibility for chapel worship. And the Bishops' Inspectors were to be in college, to satisfy themselves (we trusted) that they could assure the Bishops that the college was a proper place to train ordinands, and to make recommendations about matters we needed to take in hand and ways we might develop. To coincide with their visit, we had a meeting of the college's governing body, the trustees, on the Wednesday, with some very important decisions to make about the college's future development.

At 3.08 a.m. on the Monday at the beginning of that week (don't you look at the alarm clock when you wake like that?) I awoke as Ann was having what a neurologist later told me was a tonic-clonic seizure, or rather several of them, in which she first went rigid, than convulsed for some time, then subsided into a daze. In effect these were epileptic fits, though in Ann's case (it was eventually established) they resulted from her multiple sclerosis rather than being indications that she actually had epilepsy or some other condition which can issue in fits.

As far as I was concerned at the time, they might easily have been the convulsions of someone who was dying. But by 4.30 she was in the University Hospital and by 6.00 was in a bed in its medical admissions ward. She stayed in bed for the whole week, hardly moving a limb (voluntarily), and without its being obvious that she was ever again going to. I spent the week commuting between the hospital, the classroom and the inspectors, rather than just the last two as I had expected. On Friday afternoon I realized that on the one hand I was mentally, emotionally, and physically exhausted, but that on the other I was running at one hundred miles per hour and did not know how to stop. The departure of the inspectors removed much of the stress (not that they were difficult – rather the contrary – but the exercise is inevitably a stressful one) and I found myself able to unwind as I pottered over the weekend. The fact that my spirit made a point of searching out a 'flu bug a few days later shows that I did not unwind enough, but I tried. Those events and the story of what happened over the subsequent two years also form a significant part of the background to what follows in this book.

2

Ascent

(i)

I have long puzzled over a particular question about our relationship with God. The Bible seems to assume that our relationship with God is characterized by love and joy and enthusiasm. At the same time the great spiritual writers talk as if the development of our relationship with God can be expected to involve being more and more at home with dryness and darkness, with desert and unknowing. Is there any way of reconciling these two? I suppose the question interests me partly because I feel that my own life with God has got tougher over the years, even over the past week, but also more joyful, even over the past week. And the question more than interests me; it bothers me pastorally, because I see other people whose lives seem to get tougher without becoming more joyful. They become depressed or disillusioned or resentful instead.

What are we to expect as our lives develop? If you have known the joy of being filled with the Holy Spirit, what happens next? Just more of that? If things become tough, does it mean something is wrong? Does God give us nice feelings when we are young and expect us to live tougher when we are older? Is it the way people sometimes talk about marriage – the lovey-dovey stuff belongs to the beginning and as years go by you expect it to grow into something more solid (which is code for something more boring)? I acknowledge I am too much of a romantic to accept that lying down.

It is worth asking these questions because we need to be able to recognize what God is doing with us and to seek what God wants for us. Sometimes people find that the going gets tough and they have no way of looking at it, of looking at how God might be involved with us when things are tough. If this does not happen to us, it will happen to people we know. This experience can become something you just have to live your way through until it is over, but if that is all you do, it may not have produced its fruit.

How can our life with God be joyful and tough, be tough and joyful? The nearest I have to an answer comes in the form of a story. It is a story that will be capable of being interpreted heretically, so have mercy on it at those points. It concerns the woman of the mountains.

There was a town near the foothills of a mountain range. Living there, you could not but be aware of the reality of the mountains, though most of the people in the town ignored the mountains most of the time.

There was a woman of the mountains who would visit the town. She brought with her the smell of the mountains, the freshness, the liveliness, the strength, the awesomeness of them. There was a man who was captivated by that, and the two of them fell in love. This gave him a new kind of acquaintance with the mountains, a new kind of experience of them. It made him more aware of them. He knew that he would never be satisfied until he had climbed them.

One spring day when there were other things to do, she whispered that the time had come, and she took his hand. There was no time to buy mountain boots; he went in the sandals that he always wore in spring and summer. They walked hand-in-hand through the outskirts of the town as daffodils came out and children played and men dug their gardens, and he began to realize that he was saying goodbye. Not that he would never see the town again, but that he would never see it the same way again. Once he had been to the mountains, it would not be the same town.

On the edge of the town the highway curved away to the left, down the valley towards the coast, but as it began to curve, a dirt road continued straight ahead towards the green and earthy and purple slopes and peaks. The sounds of children and of traffic began to fade, the sound of birds and the smell of grass began to increase, and the sun warmed his back. Each quarter-hour they walked, he became more filled with a sense of well-being and happiness and a sense of love. They had their arms round each other's waists and he could feel the softness of her flesh just above her hip and could sense her fingers on the muscular hardness of his own side. He did not think he had ever been happier, and yet he knew he was only beginning a journey.

After a couple of hours the fields became woods and the dirt road became a path and started to climb. At noon they emerged from the woods to find themselves on a craggy edge from which they could look back over the way they had come. They stopped for a picnic. They talked about the mountains and about the way they had met and about their love and about this journey. And then she said they had to begin walking again. The climb was to become serious.

They were above the tree-line now and the terrain was more rugged. There was still a path, in fact there were a number of them. He suddenly realized that he could see other figures on these paths – walking a bit desultorily, it must be said. It was not clear where these paths went, and she seemed to ignore them. It was not obvious to him why her route made more sense than the other paths, but he had no alternative but to follow.

And he meant 'follow'. Previously they had walked hand-in-hand. They had strolled, really. Now she led the way. It was partly a practical thing: the way had become narrower and it was often steep and rocky, and he needed to grab hold of rocks from time to time to help him along. But besides that, she seemed to have become more decisive and dynamic, to have a more specific idea about where she wanted to take him. The playful happiness of the stroll and the picnic seemed to have quite gone. If he thought about it, the odd thing was that he had no less sense of their being together. But he did not have time to think about it much; he became too busy concentrating on the climb, on the difference between safe rocks and loose rocks, on keeping his footing on a particularly narrow ridge. He was surprised that his sandals coped with it all, but they did.

At three they again stopped for a breather, and again it was a place which gave him chance to look back to the town and back over the way they had come. They had walked for five hours, about four and three-quarters more than he was used to; he was a man who was normally insulated from the countryside by steel, glass, and rubber. The climb since lunch had taken it out of him. It was hard now to remember the light-heartedness with which they had walked through the suburbs just a few hours ago. They did not talk the way they had when they were strolling rather than climbing or the way they had over lunch. Yet he had a strange sense that their awareness of being together was at least as strong as they sat in silence. They knew that they were with each other on a crucial journey which was in its way important for her as well as for him. She so much wanted to take him to the top of the mountain where she belonged.

It was also becoming a bit hard to remember the sun on his back. He realized that this was because a mist was descending. It was cold, and as they sat there he put on his sweater.

Then she hauled him to his feet. She had never done that before: it was again as if the time for words was over for a while. For an instant she looked at him with love in her eyes, then she slapped him on the behind and turned round to begin the walk into the mist. She looked as if she knew exactly where she was going, though he was blowed if he could see how. She seemed to become even more decisive and directed than before, almost a different person from the dancing woman of the mountains who had originally won his heart. He did not mind that. It was like the unveiling of something. It did not take away from what he knew of her before, and what he knew of her before and had fallen in love with made it quite possible to trust this new tougher revelation now.

So in a strange way, as he struggled to keep up with her in the mist, he found that the love he felt in his heart was increasing in its wonder, though he did not have time to think too many romantic thoughts. Some of the time he was just wishing he had brought a thicker sweater.

At one point they had to walk along another narrow ridge, and it was a bit scary. He had no idea how far he would go if he fell. Then they had to scrabble up some steep scree, and again he did not like to think about the consequences of losing his footing. Eventually he had the chance to find out, because he did slip. And like magic she was there, knowing how to make best use of her weight to enable him to regain his balance. He remembered that story about the two pairs of footsteps becoming one, and he knew that in reality it was a fantasy. He would never be carried (actually he did not want to be). He would always have to do his own walking, but he would never be alone. And when she smiled at him for a moment as they stood, still a bit precariously, half-way across the scree, he saw love in her eyes again, and he realized how much it meant to her that he was making this journey, and he loved her back with a new kind of tenderness and commitment and fierceness that he had never felt in the little house back in the town.

In time the mist half-cleared, though not so as to make it possible to see beyond a hundred metres of where they were going or where they had been. They had that experience you have with some mountains, when ahead of you there rises another ridge and it looks to you as if this must be the last one, and you think it had better be the last one because you have climbed enough, thank you, and whose silly idea was this anyway, and why are you not playing in the street or digging the garden? But you climb it, and the reward is – another ridge to face another few hundred metres further on.

At least now that the slope was more open she could walk alongside him and make a joke or two at his expense, though she would never say whether the next ridge would be the last, and he began to wonder whether she knew, or whether this journey contained surprises for her too. But he never stopped trusting her and he never stopped loving her and thrilling at doing this walk with her and at seeing the look of love in her eyes from time to time.

They came over yet another ridge and just when he had stopped believing it could be the last . . . it was. An extraordinary vista opened out before them. The mist was quite gone and the sun was shining. They were on top of the world. Once again they could look back on the town they had come from. They could also look on in the opposite direction, and it was an extraordinary scene. They could see the layer of mist below the peak, but beyond the mountains the mist disappeared and they could gaze as far as the coast. He could see the belt of sand and the sun glinting on the waves.

But his eyes also took in the flat top of the mountain. He suddenly realized that he had not asked where they were to eat or sleep, given that it would be near evening before they reached the summit. He only realized this because as he looked across this little flat mountain top he saw a picnic laid out: blankets to sit on, a tablecloth, a basket of bread and a bottle of wine, and a man wrestling with a corkscrew.

The woman of the mountains ran to the man and they hugged and he saw the same twinkle and the same affection in the man's eyes that he loved in her eyes, and he knew this was also his father. He walked up to him shyly, but with a kind of confidence which made it possible for them to embrace, because they had her in common, and because they knew that they belonged to each other because of the love they shared from her and for her.

The three of them talked about the climb and about the forest and the scree and the mist and the dangerous moments and the falls and the ridges that never seemed to come to an end, but also about the way that it was all possible because he and she were together and because of their love for each other and because he trusted her. They ate bread and drank wine and looked in wonder over the vista. They sat in the warm silence of the evening.

And they talked about the people in the town who did not know her, and the people who did know her but who had never been drawn to climb the mountain. And they talked about the other people they had seen on the mountain. There was no one who had fallen off, no indication of fatal falls. But they had seen people who felt tempted to give up or who were on paths that would only lead to the top by a very long way round, and people who could not understand why it was such a hard climb, and people who had stopped climbing on the sunny lower slopes in order to pick daisies and enjoy the sun, or who had got stuck higher up because they found it all too hard. Each of these people seemed to be walking alone, or thought they were walking alone; they did not see themselves as walking with the woman of the mountains.

And the two with aching limbs but with love in their eyes agreed to go and tell them that they did not walk alone and to invite them to look up and see the love in the eyes of the woman of the mountains who was walking with them and who mediated and promised the presence of the one who laid the picnic feast even when it did not feel as if he was anywhere near – to invite them to look and see the love in her eyes which was for them, for you.

Below my notes for that story it says that 'following Christ is a hard road but little by little you will see the light in the darkness and drink the water which springs from a dry land – and vice versa'. I do not know where that came from; my friends sometimes add things to my files when I leave the computer switched on, and so perhaps do other angels, whether it is switched on or not.

(ii)

In theory when you come to know Christ you have found fulfilment. You have found what you were hungry for. Now, there is a song by U2 which talks about having climbed the highest mountains so as to be with God, about having run and crawled and scaled city walls, about having spoken with the tongues of angels and held the hand of the Devil, about believing that Christ broke the bonds and loosed the chains and carried the cross and all my shame . . . yet also declares that nevertheless 'I'm still running' because 'I still haven't found what I'm looking for'.

Some students were a bit bemused when I sang this song at a college gig, sounding as if I meant it. Admittedly you have to sing songs as if you mean them – at least I believe you do; but that might be why the brains behind this band told me he liked having me sing in his band because I was 'dangerous' (one of the nicest compliments I have ever been paid). But in terms of spirituality, not least, even when you have found what you were hungry for, you continue to look forward. St John of the Cross, who first made me think about the motif of the mountain because it is prominent in his own writing on spirituality, also sees us as moving through attraction and engagement to a marriage relationship with Christ, yet he still speaks of a final consummation which lies in the future.

U2 were/are high-profile Christians. Van Morrison started off as a rhythm-and-blues singer but has sung about mystical experience for nearly thirty years, since his *Astral Weeks*. His songs often refer to spiritual guides such as John Donne and William Blake. He has 'tried' a wide range of religions, and had a spell when he was thought to be a 'born-again' Christian, from which came the fine 1989 *Avalon Sunset* album (though qualifiedly commended by the magazine *Q* as 'music to fall asleep by a river by'). It included a duet with Cliff Richard about knowing that wherever we are, God's light shines on us, so that we can reach out in the deepest of confusion or despair or loneliness and find God there. But the standout track is the one which gives the album its title. With music it is often one phrase that acts as a 'hook' and has you singing it (even when you do not wish to!). I find that the same is true with words. Van sings a song about the sun setting over Avalon, a song which keeps asking 'When will I ever learn to live in God? When will I ever learn?'.

I went to the gig and bought the teeshirt and am now going to live within a few miles of Avalon. (I recently discovered that it has nothing directly to do with King Arthur but is a town on Santa Catalina Island, off the Southern California coast.)

In an interview in the *Guardian* newspaper Van Morrison was asked whether he would give up all his musical activity and expression if he could have peace of mind. He said, unhesitatingly, 'Yes'.

3

Calamity

A few months before Ann had her seizure we had been studying Job in class. The student who was living with pain of his own had asked me what the story of Job meant to me in the context of Ann's illness, and I fell into talking the class through the story of Job in the light of that. I could do it only through tears, because that is the way I am, and the student was weeping his own tears, as were one or two others who had their own pains or who identified with ours. It was the oddest teaching experience of my career. As usual I was teaching with a colleague, and one of the constructive differences between us has always been that she likes to plan everything well ahead and I like to busk. On the way out of the class she simply said, 'I wish you would tell me when you are going to do something like that' (of course the problem is that I usually do not know). I cannot remember what I said to the class and I have no notes, but I expect that what follows bears some relationship to it.

(i) Testing

Job is the story of a man who had everything, but who had that everything taken away in one of those calamities that come upon human beings. Today, three days after their death, he reminds me of Princess Diana and Dodi Fayad. In some ways their story is sadder than his. As the television said, they – or at least she – had everything but happiness, and then lost everything including their lives when they might have been on the verge of finding some happiness together.

The story of Job is told in such a way as to establish Job as a man who indeed had everything, spiritually as well as materially. He is introduced to us as a whole and upright man who worshipped God and kept well away from wrongdoing. He shows the marks of a blessed life: a big family and a prosperous household. He cared deeply about his children's spiritual state.

If you are blessed by God like that, it raises strange questions and puts strange temptations before you. What is the basis of your relationship with God? Do you keep right with God primarily because of what you get out of it? A while ago there was a thing called the prosperity gospel – I am not sure whether it still exists. On the basis of promises in the Old and New Testaments it encouraged us to believe that God intended every committed believer to expect to do well in material ways ('seek first the kingdom of God and all these things will be yours as well'). Job had proved that the prosperity gospel worked. Was he a believer only because of what he got out of it?

And what about God? God was the beneficiary of Job's commitment, worship, and sacrifices. It is rather nice to have someone committed to you, serving you, worshipping you, giving you meals. That raises strange questions about God and puts strange temptations before God. What is the basis of God's relationship with Job? Is Job blessed only for what God can get out of it? Is the arrangement between God and Job a purely collusive contract – you scratch my back and I'll scratch yours? Is it a business contract rather than a personal relationship?

One way to discover whether that is so is for one party to fail to keep their side of the contract. People often assume that our relationship with God is like that. If we make a slip in our relationship with God, God is quick to abandon us. Here the question is raised the other way round. What if God abandons Job? The opening scene in the story of Job is a dramatization of that question.

Strange things happen in this scene, and one is not sure how much theology to derive from it. I presume that the story of Job as a whole is based on something that actually happened, but the

opening scene takes place in heaven, not on earth. It must issue
from human imagination or divine revelation; it cannot be mere
ordinary human reporting. It pictures a scene in heaven where
Yahweh sits in court with 'the sons of God', the other heavenly
beings who participate in the taking of decisions on what is to
happen in the world, and in the implementing of those decisions.
They gather to give account of their work. One of them is called
the 'Adversary'. The Hebrew word is satan, but the word is not
someone's name, like the later name Satan. Like the English word
'adversary' it is an ordinary if rare and poetic word for an
opponent (an opponent in battle or in court); it occurs a number
of times in the Psalms in this connection. It is also used of a
heavenly figure in Zechariah 3 and 1 Chronicles 21. Both passages
hint at the possibility that the Adversary enters into his work with
excessive enthusiasm.

In Job the role the Adversary plays in the scene in heaven is to
raise the kind of sharp questions which will safeguard against the
possibility that the relationship between God and Job is contrac-
tual and collusive. In the British parliament the opposition party
can be referred to as 'Her Majesty's loyal opposition'. They serve
queen and country by asking pressing questions of the majority
party, making sure it does not have too easy a time, and making
it harder for it to pursue extreme policies. In this scene in heaven,
the Adversary fulfils a role which is at once negative and positive.
It is negative because of the suspiciousness it presupposes and the
trouble it brings, but it is positive because of its potential to
vindicate both human beings and God.

The whole presentation thus differs from the presentation of
Satan in some parts of the New Testament, though it is not so
different from that in the story of Jesus' testing in the wilderness
and in Jesus' reference to Satan's testing of Peter. The nearest I have
to an understanding of the relationship between the presentation
of these figures is as follows.

In Revelation Satan is identified with the serpent in Genesis 3.
Now Genesis 3 offers no hint that the serpent is a supernatural
figure. The information that Satan was at work behind the serpent
is information that Revelation adds to Genesis. In reading Genesis

3 we need to bring that fact in, but we must not do that too early. We can easily obscure what God meant us to learn from Genesis 3 itself with its picture of suggestions coming to Eve through an earthly creature with the symbolic attributes of a serpent, such as wisdom and danger.

In the same way the New Testament indicates that the figure of Satan stands behind the figure of the Adversary in Job 1, and in due course we need to bring that in, but again we must not do that too early. We can easily obscure what God meant us to learn from Job 1 itself with its portrait of a heavenly being who serves God precisely by asking suspicious questions and proposing drastic testings. It is God, after all, who invites the Adversary to evaluate Job, as it is the Spirit who drives Jesus into the wilderness to be tested by Satan.

If the scene in heaven places some theological pressure on us, the resultant scene on earth places more. Who is this God who allows servants to be killed, animals to be slaughtered, and a family to be devastated, and then allows a man to suffer terrible illness and a wife to break down as she watches it, all to prove a theological point? The theological and moral pressure may seem to be reduced if we declare that the scene in heaven and the scene on earth are equally the product of human imagination; they are part of a parable. They are fiction. Yet we may also lose out by appealing to that possibility. For the fact is that employees do lose their lives in the course of doing their jobs, animals are the victims of human greed and natural disasters, and families do get wiped out in terrible accidents. This is not fiction but fact. The question is, how does God relate to those events?

Much of me wishes to disassociate God from them, at least as their cause. I want God to notice when such things happen, I want God to grieve, I want God to comfort, I want God to be able to take the pieces of the shattered jigsaw and do something with them. But what kind of God would be their cause?

Job raises the question of what kind of God would not be their cause. There is a famous conundrum which suggests that the fact of evil indicates that God cannot be both wholly good and wholly

sovereign in the world. Either God is wholly responsible for all
that happens but not wholly good (which explains the bad things
that happen to good people). Or God is wholly good but is not in
a position to ensure that only good things happen to good people
because of having allowed other beings (including human beings
and Satan himself) to have power in the world,.

My impression is that Christians regularly opt for the second
of these solutions to the conundrum. The Job story points to the
first solution. Whereas modern Christians prefer a God who is
very nice but not very efficient, the Job story offers us a God who
does some pretty odd things but who is at least clearly in charge.
Even though that does raise questions about God's goodness,
questions which are the very concerns of the book we are considering, there is some security in it. I am simultaneously frightened
and reassured by the fact that God accepts responsibility for the
trouble that comes to us, for the disasters to working people and
the suffering of animals and the calamities that come upon
families and the pain that comes to individuals and the friction
which that pain then causes between couples.

We are told that the story of Job as it unfolds on earth has a
prior history in heaven. By definition this particular history is
not universalizable. Job is a test case. What happens to him
happens because he is not like everyone else, because he is not
Mr Average-spirituality. He is Mr Super-spirituality (as the story
will go on to make even more clear). We cannot infer from the
explanation of his suffering an explanation of ours. Yet what
we may be able to infer is that calamities do have explanations,
even if we do not know what they are. For there is another
feature of the story of Job which delights me every time I think
about it, not least because it establishes a similarity between Job
and us. It is that Job himself never knows about chapters 1 and
2 of 'his' book. So he goes through his pain the same way as we
do. And he illustrates how the fact that we do not know what
might explain our suffering, what purpose God might have in
it, does not constitute the slightest suggestion that this suffering
has no explanation. After all, Job could never have dreamt of
the explanation of what happened to him.

I cannot imagine the story which makes it OK for God to have made Ann go through what she has been through. But I can imagine that there is such a story. I do not know whether we will ever know what that story is. Job and his wife did not come to know his story, and Job was apparently rebuked for insisting that he should know. Thinking about this now has made me repent again of my periodic attempts to confront God over the question (which anyway work no more for me than they did for Job).

(ii) Prayer

'Are you still holding on to your integrity? Curse God and die.' One can imagine a little bit of the pain that lies behind Mrs Job's exhortation, the only words she utters in this story. She has been the wife of the man who had everything. If we presuppose no questioning of the realities of a patriarchal society on her part (there is a feminist reading of Job, but she lived too soon to read it), that makes her the woman who had everything: a successful husband, a fruitful womb, an impressive household, a happy grown-up family. She, too, sees everything collapse. Perhaps she loved Job and perhaps the two of them could have survived the loss of possessions and even the terrible death of her children, until the pain of seeing him physically afflicted became too much. Then she just wanted to end it all, wanted him to end it all. 'Curse God and die' – provoke God to send your own thunderbolt.

I may be forgiven for wondering whether in some respects putting up with the pain of someone near you is trickier than putting up with your own. At least, it raises some trickinesses of its own. When it is yours, it is yours, and you get on with it. You have the responsibility. The handling of it lies in your hands. When it is someone else's you are simply helpless, and you may feel guilty, too, for being able to do nothing. As I feel that in relation to Ann's loss, so I can sometimes sense our friends' feeling it in relation to mine as well as to hers, and I can imagine that they also feel a kind of helplessness over it, whereas for me it is something I just have to get on with handling.

Job gets on with handling it. His servants are killed and his animals are slaughtered and his children are dead. With almost indecent apparent deliberateness he grieves and he mourns and he kneels, and he praises the name of Yahweh. Physically afflicted from head to toe, he rebukes his wife for expecting that we should receive good from God and not calamity. Who is this man?

Fortunately he does not exist. In due course he breaks. He will not curse God, as his wife suggested, but he does curse his life. And he begins to ask those questions to which he will not receive answers, even though there are answers he could have been given, questions which all begin with the word 'Why?' They are 'Why?' questions about himself (Why was I not stillborn?) which become generalized into 'Why' questions about people in pain in general (Why is life given to people in misery?).

People's 'Why?' questions are sincere, but one suspects that they are not to be taken too literally. I am not sure how much it would have helped Job to have chapters 1–2 told to him at this point. I am not clear that he would have responded, 'Oh, I see, that's OK then.' I have implied that some answers would be welcome. That is because meaninglessness is hard to cope with. The fear felt by his friends, to whom we will come shortly, is that everything is meaningless if Job's story is as it looks. Any inadequate answer to the problem of suffering is preferable to the honest and true answer 'We do not know', which is why people go around repeating inadequate answers. They reassure us that there is meaning after all.

But Job's problem (and mine) is not just puzzlement but tiredness. When he asks why he was not stillborn, this is not because he wants an answer, but because it would mean peace, sleep, rest. When people ask 'Why?', we have to ask what is the question behind the question rather than give them an inadequate answer to the question which was not the real question.

I have a strange memory from when I was about thirteen. We used to have to walk a few hundred metres from the school building to the sports pavilion. One afternoon, for some reason I undertook to carry everyone's rugby kit from the main building to the pavilion (I cannot remember whether it was fifteen or thirty,

one team's or two teams'). We all had our kit in drawstring bags
and the strings were all put over my head so that the bags hung
down all round me. The thing I remember is the extraordinary
feeling of lightness when I took them all off. It was like walking
on the moon (except that no one had yet done that).

The memory sometimes comes back to me as a metaphor. For
the last decade I have carried two sets of kit. One is the burden
of Ann's illness (it is not really the burden of Ann, of course). It
is partly a burden of responsibility. In our house, it is I who have
to see that the decisions get taken and implemented, whether it is
what we are to have for supper or whether we move to America.
In one sense that is no worse than it is for a single person, though
I am having to make decisions for two. (We visited some long-
standing friends a while ago, and one of them commented on the
fact that I had to think for two people; I had not quite noticed,
but I could see what he meant, and it was helpful to see it.) It is
even more like being a single parent, but with the extra dimension
of the ambiguity of the fact that one of the people I am trying to
think for is an adult who has an adult's right to be involved in the
process.

The other burden is the responsibility of being the principal of
a theological college. I could not ask for a more collaboratively
inclined team of colleagues and I know that in the end it is God's
college not mine, but the fact that I am paid more than the rest is
a symbol of the fact that humanly-speaking there is in the end one
person who is humanly responsible for ensuring that the college's
spiritual life is sound, the courses are good, creative new ideas are
generated and the finances break even, and that person is me.
When I said I was leaving, one of the college children asked if it
would therefore cease to be called 'St John's College', and that
expresses the point.

Most of the time I do not feel that these responsibilities are a
burden. I love Ann and I love my work. It is when I put the
responsibilities down that I realize that they are a heavy weight.
In 1996 we had a fortnight in the Alps with two friends. Early on
we had a late-night conversation which somehow turned into a
discussion of whether we looked forward to death, and two of us

agreed that it was an attractive prospect because it meant putting burdens down. It meant we could just lie there. Over the fortnight, however, I forgot about college, and these two friends shared responsibility for Ann, and I realized it was like putting the rugby bags down. I felt lighter, like moon-walking.

Job's cursing and his longing for rest are but the beginning of chapter after chapter of questioning and challenging that dominate his book. They constitute more than a third of it. They continue to ask questions, but these are often patently rhetorical – they are questions that conceal statements. 'Do I have any power to help myself?' 'Does not humanity have hard service on earth?' They express longings. 'If only my anguish could be weighed.' 'Oh that God would be willing to let loose his hand and cut me off.' They issue challenges, to God as well as to human beings. 'Will you never look away from me?' They make requests, though that is too mild a word. 'Tell me what charges you have against me.' 'Stop frightening me.' They make statements, sometimes as outrageous as the questions and the longings and the challenges and the requests. 'If I hold my head high, you stalk me like a lion.' 'God has wronged me.'

The straightness of Job's speech recalls that of the Psalms which pour out human grief, pain, anger, and abandonment, and Job as a whole has been compared to a huge psalm of lament. It is characteristic of those psalms that they display an extraordinary freedom in what they assume we may legitimately say to God, and Job takes that freedom to its logical extreme. There is apparently no limit to what you can say to God. God can take it.

To judge from the end of the book, God does not merely tolerate it, but rejoices in it. Another feature of this story that delights me every time I read it is the moment when God comments on the fact that Job has spoken the truth about God, as his friends have not. We have listened to chapter after chapter of Job's storming at God and storming about God, assaulting God and attempting any which way to get God to speak, and we have listened to God eventually tearing strips off Job and putting him in his place and Job perhaps accepting that, and then we overhear the declaration that actually Job has been speaking the truth about God.

There is a scheme for understanding the way we grow as human beings that sees us as moving through orientation, disorientation, and new orientation – not once and for all, but on an ongoing basis. Orientation means you know how life works, you know who God is, you know who you are, you know how you and life and God relate. Disorientation is what takes place when that knowledge gets shattered for some reason: your marriage breaks up or you lose a child or you lose your job or you study theology and discover questions you did not know existed. Renewed orientation involves a fresh understanding which does justice both to your original perspective and to what shattered it. The story of Job takes him through that three-stage process, and the argument between him and his friends is about how you cope with disorientation.

The friends cope with it by denying it, as people often do when they refuse to acknowledge the reality of loss and grief and questions. The friends insist on fitting what has happened to Job within the framework of what they thought they already knew about the way God relates to us and runs the world. In that framework, calamity is intelligible. It respects known parameters. The emphasis of Eliphaz, Bildad and Zophar, repeated until it annoys us almost as much as it annoys Job and God, is that people who live right in relation to God find blessing, while people who do not do that experience trouble. When calamity comes, we thus have to ask whether it constitutes chastisement for our wrongdoing, as Paul declares is the case with some people's trouble at Corinth (see 1 Corinthians 11:30). The nuance brought by the angry young man Elihu is that calamity is designed to bring us to repentance for wrongdoing, to draw us back to God, to make it possible for us to grow in our relationship with God. It is related to Paul's understanding of his own experience in 2 Corinthians 12, which Eugene Peterson's *The Message* paraphrases as follows:

> Because of the extravagance of these revelations, and so I wouldn't get a big head, I was given the gift of a handicap to keep me in constant touch with my limitations. . . . At first I didn't think of it as a gift, and begged God to remove it. Three times I did that, and then he told me, 'My grace is enough'.

Another of the delightful features of the story of Job is that his friends are not wrong in living by this theology, as its reappearance in Paul shows. Indeed Job's own story illustrates this very theology. In the end the person who lives right in relation to God does find blessing, and the person who experiences calamity is brought to repentance and led on in his relationship to God by his experience. That is so by the end; it is involved in Job's finding the new orientation which also does justice to the old.

But the point of the argument between Job and his friends is to demonstrate that that old orientation does not survive being set against Job's current experience. The friends, or at least Eliphaz, Bildad and Zophar, will not recognize this. Rather than revise their theology (as a student once put it in an essay for me) they rewrite Job's life. In contrast, the reason why God commends Job is that Job insists on facing facts rather than hiding from them. Job curses and argues and confronts and challenges and insists and scorns, all in the cause of a resolute requirement that facts be faced rather than evaded. He has lived right by God; what has happened to him does not fit that, and he would like to know how he is supposed to fit that into his universe.

There is a myth about a Greek villain called Procrustes who forced his victims to fit the bed he gave them. If they were too short for it, he stretched them on a rack, if too tall, he cut off the overhang. We may be tempted to make the orientation offered by the story of Job as a whole the Procrustean bed into which we make everyone's experience fit, as if the point of the book is to provide the missing piece from the jigsaw of the problem of suffering: we now have the answer. There are a number of ways of understanding calamity when it comes to us: it may be punishment for wrongdoing (Eliphaz, Bildad and Zophar), or it may be designed to take us on in our relationship with God (Elihu), or it may be designed to vindicate our relationship with God (the opening and closing scenes). The question is, which one applies?

But that is to miss the point, a point to which attention is drawn by Job's continuing unawareness of what happened in chapters 1–2. It is to refuse disorientation. It is to think that we have the problem solved. It reminds me of the preacher who closed his sermon about the Pharisee and the Publican by thanking God that we are not like the Pharisee. We have missed the point. The story of Job suggests that there may sometimes be explanations for calamity which we do not know, but we have to live with God without knowing them.

(iii) Trust

Job is a postmodern book. It does not move in linear fashion from the question to the answer. It walks round the question over 42 chapters, worrying at it, trying out ideas, looking at it from different angles, and then leaves you. In one sense you are no further forward in chapter 42; as I have suggested, it ends up reaffirming the theology which was implicit in its beginning and was explicit on the lips of Eliphaz, Bildad and Zophar. The great speech in chapters 38–41 with which Yahweh confronts Job must in some sense be the book's climax, but when I have told students how it does that, I have not been sure I have convinced myself.

In that great double speech Yahweh first takes Job on a great tour of creation, as if to say 'Are you old enough to have been there when I created all this, or to have had time in your life to look at all of it? And are you big enough to control it?' Another of the delights of the book (though this time a puzzling one) is that in this *pièce de résistance*, there is actually little that has not in principle already been said somewhere in the book by Yahweh or by Job or by one of the friends. In this *tour de force* it is said with huge and relentless power, but that undermines rather than vindicates the submission of Job in 40:1–5. One has the impression that Job surrenders because he is overwhelmed by superior firepower rather than because he is morally or intellectually convinced by an argument. The man who wanted to talk man-to-man with God now wants to get away.

What is the point of God's three-page series of questions? They actually have several points. They begin with whether the world is under control. Job has been challenging God about whether there is order in the world. God challenges Job about whether he is in a position to come to a judgment on such questions. God was there when the world was created and given its stability, regularity and order, when potential forces of disorder and death had their bounds and purpose set. Was Job? In his confrontation of God Job has insisted on arguing on equal terms with God. God's speech is a relentless insistence that Job is too small and the world too big for Job to pretend to be in that position. Job had implied that the world ought to be intelligible in terms which make him the centre. God denies Job's Job-centred, or rather humanity-centred, understanding of the world. The world itself is manifestly not exclusively centred on humanity and its needs. So the presupposition of Job's challenge to God was mistaken. The world works the way it does in order to fulfil a broader (we might say, more ecological) agenda, in a sense just to be itself.

Sometimes I find that a long car drive gives me an opportunity to talk things out with God. I am not very good at quiet days and the like, but there is no way of hastening the end of a long drive (well, there is a way, and my friends usually claim that I take it). On a recent car journey I was talking through things with God, and I went on to challenge God about Ann. I said, 'You have to have mercy on her.' In response God chillingly echoed back to me my own words, saying, 'I will have mercy on whom I will have mercy': more chilling in their context in Romans 9:15, I think, than when uttered by Moses in Exodus 33:19. In other words, 'What I do with Ann is my business. You can trust me with Ann or not, as you like. It makes little difference to me. It's between me and her, not me and you. I decline to be held to account by you for Ann.' I was being treated the way Job was treated.

With further irony, once God has Job by the lapels (the reverse of the stance Job had been looking for), God has no intention of letting go easily. Job gives in, hoping to escape, but finds that instead God starts off again; one can almost hear Job's desperate 'Oh no!'. God's second speech is shorter, but it does seem to say something new, and something quite relevant to my challenge about Ann. Job had been questioning God's fairness, God's justice. It is the classic question about theodicy, about the justice of God. God's second response is, 'OK, if you are so clever and so committed to things being fair, you set about running the world for a while. Put pride down. Dethrone oppression. Then I will acknowledge you.'

'And I am prepared to be evaluated by my own criteria,' God goes on. 'I invite you to look at the evidence that I can be trusted to run the world in a fashion that works things out fairly.' God develops this claim in a different way from the one that we see in the first speech. There God painted on a broad canvas, took Job on a lightning tour. Here God is David Attenborough focusing in a whisper on just two creatures. In Hebrew they are behemoth and leviathan. The words could refer to ordinary animals (ordinary in one sense but extraordinary in another), the hippopotamus and the crocodile, the most fearsome creatures you might ever expect to meet in Palestine. But these words come to be used for more mythical creatures like the dragon, creatures which symbolize the powers of chaos and disorder which ever seem to threaten to overwhelm the life of the cosmos and our individual lives. Set Job alongside either of these creatures, and if he is wise he will run a mile. He cannot pretend to control them.

God's relationship to them is quite different. He is behemoth's maker, who can approach him with a sword (40.19). He can treat leviathan as a pet (41.5). God had, after all, specifically formed leviathan to frolic in the seas (Psalm 104.26), as much a joke as the Loch Ness Monster. Job knows about God's relationship with creation and the powers of disorder within it. He is invited to assume that this expresses God's relationship with the forces of disorder in his life, too. That is the only answer he is going to get to the problem of evil. It is the answer he already has. God has demonstrated the capacity to keep the forces of disorder under control. Job has to assume that God is still doing that, even when he cannot see that this is so. He has to trust even when he cannot see.

Job's response, especially in its closing words, is enigmatic. According to the traditional translations Job despises himself and repents in dust and ashes. But literally he says, 'I despise and repent [change my mind or feel sorry] over dust and ashes': there is no word for 'myself' and the preposition means 'over' not 'in'.

Since God is about to comment on how truly Job has spoken, the traditional translation seems a poor way to make sense of his laconic words. Perhaps he is announcing his intention to climb out of the ash heap in the light of those reminders that God has the power and that God makes a commitment to seeing that things work out. Even though he still cannot make theological sense of what has happened, he accepts that he must trust even when he cannot understand, and he determines to do so.

4

Cheek

Some while ago I remember being puzzled when I read one or two books about preaching, because they had chapters in them on titles for sermons. I had never felt the need of a title for a sermon. Then on a visit to the USA I think I discovered the answer. In small-town America local newspapers used to, and may still, carry advertisements stating not only the times of next Sunday's services but also the subjects of the sermons. It seemed to me a wondrous expectation that not only should you have a striking title for the sermon, but that you should have it by the Wednesday before you were due to preach it. Both of these I would normally find difficult.

If this were next Sunday's sermon, at last I would be able to fulfil the requirement, because this chapter is about 'five amazing things that you can tell God not to do'. This subject is partly related to a sermon a colleague of mine once preached about the ten bad habits of God (God is always late, is unpredictable, does not care what people think, has a love which is blind, prefers the broken to the strong, is self-contradictory, does not remember evil and personally repents of evil, is faithful but has changes of mind, is paradoxical, and behaves like a child).

The five amazing things you can tell God not to do are found in a prayer of Moses in Exodus 32. There is Moses on the top of the mountain with God, receiving instructions about how God and Israel are to relate to each other and what is to be the pattern of worship. There at the bottom of the mountain is Israel itself, rather impatient about how long Moses is delaying at the top of this mountain and deciding that it will exercise some creative initiative, indulge in some innovative liturgical development, in connection with the question of how God and Israel will relate and how Israel will worship. Ironically, Israel at the bottom of the mountain is doing exactly the opposite to what God is telling Moses at the top of the mountain. It leads Moses into having to pray for the people.

First, he says, 'Don't lose your temper.' 'Why should your anger burn against your people, whom you brought out of Egypt with great power and a mighty hand?'

It seems strange to think of God getting angry. There are at least two important and precious implications in the fact that God does so. One is that it means that God is a real person. God is someone with feelings and passions such as compassion and mercy. God is someone who loves and cares, who joys and delights, who gets jealous and gets angry. God is not a kind of abstract entity up there on the top of the mountain or an impassive monarch sitting on a throne in heaven, untouched by anything. God is not an idea, nor merely the ground of my being. God is a person with passions, and therefore among the passions are anger, wrath, and a temper to lose. And that is part of God's being, in whose image we are made.

It is easy for doctrine to turn God into something you study. God becomes a matter of ideas. You wrestle with understanding the idea of God being One yet also being Three and the whole business becomes something abstract. But studying doctrine can also become a way we understand more about God the person. We can think about God having three ways of being God, all of them ways that relate to us.

Our church has a community centre, and I remember once discussing her job with the then warden. She knew that as warden she needed to have her finger on what was going on in the community centre as a whole and on its policies. She also needed to hang around the mums' and toddlers' group and the lunch club, so that she was involved and not remote. Of course she could not do both of these at once. If she was involved with particular mums all the time, a crisis could develop elsewhere or some key policy questions could be neglected.

God is like and unlike our warden. God needs to have a finger on the world as a whole but also to be involved with nations, communities, churches and individuals. God can do both because God is One, but has three ways of being God – Father, Son and Spirit. An old way to think of this is to think of the Son and the Spirit as the two arms of God. One arm was extended at the incarnation, once and for all. The other is extended forever in the world and in the church. The effect of extending two arms, as opposed to none or one, is to make an embrace possible. We are invited by God's two arms to live 'in' God: within the embrace of Father, Son and Spirit. That is what God's being Trinity makes possible.

God is a person, and the doctrine of the Trinity is designed among other things to safeguard that fact and to show how God can be personal in relation to us. It is not an enigma to be explained but a description to be appreciated. It is also because of being a person that God gets angry.

I suspect that the Israelites talked about God being angry because that was often how it seemed to be, to judge from what happened to them. You know when someone is angry with you: if your ear is cuffed, you know there is probably some reason for this. Things go wrong in your life, or in the world, or in the church, and you infer that God must be angry. Then you either try to infer the rational explanation for that, and repent, or you conclude that there is no rational explanation, and you say, 'Come on, stop it,' as Job did.

If we look at the world and the church as we know it, it would be a reasonable inference that God is angry. Perhaps that is why the world and church (in Europe, at least) are in such a mess. We easily accept the fact that the church is so weak and insignificant and shrug our shoulders, instead of asking whether God is angry. What we should be doing is challenging God about letting the church be the laughing-stock of the nation, as it often seems to be. Instead, we simply accept it or make excuses, or try to do our best, our really pathetic best, to do something about it. Perhaps what we should be doing is what Moses does, saying to God, 'Why are you losing your temper?' We might even get a response.

Moses' second challenge to God is, 'Don't give up on us'. Don't give up on the project that you have begun. 'Why should your anger burn against your people, whom you have brought out of Egypt with great power and a mighty hand?' You have only started the job. You said you were going to take us into the land you promised us. You said that you were going to enter into a relationship with us. You said that you were going to provide the world with a model of what it was like to be the people of Yahweh. You are not going to give up on the job, are you? You are not going to give up on us, are you? You can't do that.

Again I suggest that if we look at a world and a church where it can seem as if God has given up on us, then Moses' kind of prayer may be one we should be praying. Why give up on the church? One can think of umpteen reasons for doing so. 'But don't give up on the church. The job is only half done, Lord.'

'Don't give up on me.' I would give up on me. Moses invites us to challenge God about giving up when the task is only half-completed, with regard to the world, the church, or individuals such as ourselves.

Moses' third challenge is, 'Don't give the wrong impression.' It continues from the second. 'Why should the Egyptians say, "It was with evil intent that Yahweh brought them out, to kill them in the mountains and to wipe them off the face of the earth." ' Think of the kind of impression you would be conveying to the world, to the whole of creation. Think of your own reputation.

This is one of the standard bases upon which prayers in the Bible appeal to God. We ask God to do things 'for God's glory'; that might seem a somewhat selfish basis of appeal. It is 'for your name's sake', lest people think badly of you. The people in the Bible are totally unscrupulous in prayer. They will do anything to get God to do the things that are near God's own heart and God's own agenda, to get God motivated to act. 'You cannot cast us off at this moment and give the impression that you could not do the job after all, that you were not capable of bringing a people into a relationship with yourself and into their promised land, even if you were capable of bringing them out of Egypt.'

And 'Don't be inflexible.' Turn from your fierce anger. Change your mind and do not bring disaster on your people. The Old Testament is not at all afraid of the notion of God having a change of mind. Readers of the Bible worry about this too, as if God should not have to do a thing like that. Perhaps part of the explanation for God's willingness to have a change of mind is this: Anyone who is involved in leadership knows that most of the time the kinds of decisions that you are taking are not made on the basis of this being one-hundred-per-cent obviously the right action, or even ninety-per-cent obviously the right action. They are often made on a sixty-forty basis, if you are lucky, or 51-49. And God is in the same position as anyone else with regard to this. God is always having to choose between the least calamitous courses of action.

So it does not take much to push God from 51 to 49. God had decided to do this, but was only a percentage point away from doing the other. 'Could you not reconsider the basis on which you have made that decision? Could you not just change those figures around? Don't be the kind of person who, once they have made a decision, won't reconsider.' Politicians let themselves be caught in a bind in this way, as if changing one's mind is a weakness. Being prepared to change your mind is a strength (well, admittedly, not if you do it all the time). To be flexible is a strength. And one of the things that is going on in prayer is that we are indeed asking God to do something different from what God was going to do. Indeed, if that is not part of what is going on in prayer, then there is no point in prayer. The point of this kind of prayer is to get God to do something that otherwise God would not do, or not to do something that otherwise God would do. When we are asking God to do things, it is an activity that is designed to make a difference. We are saying to God 'Don't be inflexible. Change your mind. Do something different from what you intended.'

Ann and I once invited a friend of ours to come on holiday with us, and she declined because she could not really afford it and she did not want to come without paying every penny of her way. The next year she could afford it and came, and we also invited another friend. This second friend seemed likely to decline for the same reason, but our first friend urged us to try to persuade her, not to take 'No' for an answer. I expostulated, 'But you wouldn't come last year!' 'You didn't try to persuade me,' she said. I had given in, taken 'No' for an answer. I would not do it again with her, or with God.

Fifthly, 'Don't forget your word.' 'Remember your servants Abraham, Isaac and Israel, to whom you swore by your own self: "I will make your descendants as numerous as the stars in the sky and I will give your descendants all this land I promised them, and it will be their inheritance for ever." '

God has made some promises and what Moses is doing in prayer is reminding God of these promises. Talk of 'claiming' things from God can sound questionable, but there is something to it. You are battering on God's door or on God's chest and saying, 'We will not allow you to forget the words that you have uttered to us about your intentions. We will not allow you to forget your promises.' What we are doing in prayer is reminding God of commitments that God has undertaken, that God cannot get off the hook.

And Yahweh had a change of mind about the disaster that was planned for the people. If we want to be philosophical (in a certain sort of way), of course, we can say that God knew ahead of time that the moment would come for a change of mind and that it was all part of a plan. We may prefer to safeguard God's sovereignty in this way. But the Bible does not do so. More often what the Bible does is lay the story out as a story, lay it out in narrative order, lay it out as history. It then portrays God's response to Moses as a real response. We are not told, in brackets, 'Now of course God knew ahead of time that Moses would pray that way, and God had made allowance for that.' If this had been so, would

God's response really have been a response? In the story the Bible tells, it was a real response. What is going on in prayer is that God is involving us in the process of decision-making whereby things happen in the world. It is not the case that God decided by fiat ahead of time, before Day Six of Creation as it were, what was to happen in each of the umpteen trillion years that was now to unfold. It is the case that God decided to create some people who would be made in God's image, with the characteristics of God, and would then be drawn into the project that God was initiating at the moment of creation. And prayer is one of the ways in which they would be drawn into the fulfilment of that project in the world. That is why, if we do not say things in prayer, things do not happen. Perhaps that is why history has gone on for such a long time. That is why church history has gone on for such a long time. That is why Israel's history went on for such a long time. God never found that anyone suggested the right action at the right moment. God invites us into the fulfilment of that divine purpose in the world. Thus, when people pray, things happen (or get prevented from happening).

Normally the way prayer goes on in the church bears no relation to what the Bible has to say about the subject, like most other things that go on in the church.

So there are five amazing things you can tell God not to do:

- Don't lose your temper
- Don't give up with the job half done
- Don't give people the excuse to misjudge you
- Don't be inflexible
- Don't forget your promises.

Or to express these five daring exhortations as positives:

- Be patient with us
- Be persistent with us
- Be aware of what people think
- Be prepared to change your mind
- Be mindful of your promises.

5

Community

When people ask me what I think we will miss in moving to the USA, they often comment on the difficulty of leaving a place where you have lived for twenty-seven years. Neither the geographical place nor the length of time seem particular issues for me, though I am prepared to discover that I am wrong. I do expect to miss working, living, and worshipping in the kind of community to which I have belonged – I would miss it even if we had only been here for five years. I will especially miss it because it has been such a supportive context for Ann and me as we have lived with Ann's illness, all the more so with the particular pressures of the last few years.

From time to time I have heard people complain that a college is not a community. They have said this in anger and in anguish. In our college I think I have heard it less in recent years, and that is probably in part something to do with Ann, with the role she plays in focusing the community for some people. Indeed, there is a significant contrast between that protest and the contents of the following note which a student wrote to me when (all unbeknown to him) we were in the midst of wondering whether it was time to leave.

For the last five or six weeks I have been praying for you. I think this has come from my struggling with questions about what community is. My conclusions are that there is a huge pressure from secular society's values on colleges, which can cause conflict for the community and therefore conflict for you. The Church (as an institution) is

affected by these values and therefore unwittingly demands some of
them be part of our college – i.e. more authority and stratification
etc. – therefore putting more demands on you. Even my own presup-
positions and insecurities want these values, when I am not close to
God.

I therefore would like to say that I feel we are living as a biblical
community, i.e. a type of corporate prophecy. The balance we have
to have here is that we do not lose the secular part of ourselves but
struggle and transform it by the openness of our community. We
students feel we can be honest and not judged. If we can be honest,
we can live in truth.

I also realize that with a prophetic community goes rejection,
uncertainty, and a desert. Perhaps this is why I feel I need to pray for
you.

As I have implied, I do not feel that kind of pressure anywhere
near as much now as I once did, and I suspect that Ann is the key
to that. But the student is right that there is a strong tension within
many of us between a desire for a oneness in Christ which denies
hierarchies and a desire for the security of having somebody in
charge who will exercise strong leadership, and he is right that
the former is God's ideal vision for the church (and the world, for
that matter). I confess that I worry a bit about people who are
quite willing to carry the burden of leadership for ever, who are
even enthusiastic about it. Jotham's parable in Judges 9 wisely
reminds us that the best leaders are probably not the people who
want the job.

(i)

Being able to utter the complaint that 'a college is not a community' presupposes various things: that we know what a community
is, that a college ought to be one, and that this is important. The
second and third of those I believe – a college ought to be a
community and this is important. The first assumption, that we
know what a community is, is trickier.

A few years ago a sociology lecturer told me about some research that had been done into the essence of community, the nature of community, the real meaning of the word. It was found that there was nothing you could identify as the real meaning of the word except that it was a 'warm' word, it suggested something nice. And of course that was underlying the anguish when people said that a college was not a community. They were saying they were cold, if you like. And it also explains the degree to which the word community is used; in a political context, for instance, we talk about the local community and community tax and the European Community and the international community and the community of faiths and even the world community. It is a word with such a wide range of meanings that to say that a church or a college or an area is a community, or that it is not, must be nonsense until we have said what we mean by the word in this context. Ever since hearing of that research I have avoided using the word, and have felt no deprivation; avoiding clichés is usually an aid to clear thinking. How can we begin to define community?

Psalm 111 gives us some of the markers of a community. Not surprisingly the first feature of community life that it points to is worship. It is a psalm, so that would be so, would it not? In fact, some psalms do begin in other ways, so maybe it is worth noting that this one begins with worship. 'Hallelu-yah', it starts. 'Praise Yahweh.' The verb is plural. Praise is something the psalm challenges people to do together. But then immediately it changes to the singular – 'I will praise Yahweh with my whole heart.' Then straightaway that individual worship is once more set in the context of the community – 'I will praise Yahweh in the company of the upright and among the congregation.' So the psalmist believes that the deeply felt worship of the individual is really important; but in the way the sentence works, that individual worship is set in the context of the worship of the community.

That might suggest various insights. It might hint that we cannot evaluate the full significance of our individual worship unless we can see how it feeds into corporate worship. It might also hint that the reality of corporate worship depends on the reality of individuals worshipping at the heart of it.

Because this is a psalm it points us to worship as the first feature of the community to which the psalmist belongs. Worship is not the thing anybody spends most of their time doing, even in a convent. But worship is the framework, the heart, and the key to what the church, at least, is and does as a community.

The second feature of the life of the psalmist's community that we hear of in Psalm 111 is study. As is the case with worship, that clearly fits the kind of community I have belonged to, but significantly the psalm is implying that it also fits other kinds of community. 'The works of Yahweh are great, studied by all who take delight in them' (verse 2). Maybe that has already been hinted in verse 1 when the psalmist speaks of worshipping with the whole heart, because in the Bible the heart is not just the centre of the emotions. In fact, if you want to talk biblically about your emotions, you are as likely to speak in terms of your stomach or your kidneys ('Darling, I love you with all my kidneys'). The heart is the centre of the whole person as a thinker and not just as someone with feelings. It is the locus of the mind. So the worship that the psalm speaks of is one which occupies the psalmist's whole mind. 'I will praise the Lord with my whole mind.' It is exactly the determination Paul urges on the Corinthians (see 1 Cor. 14:15).

In the common life of a theological college the feeding of the mind probably occupies more time than any other single occupation apart from sleep. Sometimes the two coincide, of course. In a fellowship group we were once each asked to think of the word which best described our life at that moment, and one person wrote 'a sponge'. That summed it up rather vividly. Come to the worship of the community, says the psalmist, and squeeze your sponge out to the glory of God, make it material for praise, pour it all out to God, and then go and fill it some more. 'I will praise the Lord with my whole mind.'

'The works of Yahweh are great, and studied by all who take delight in them.' The works are the great acts which God has done in Israel's story. The psalm goes on to recall the way God brought the people out of Egypt, the way God was revealed to them at Sinai, the way they knew God's provision in the wilderness, the way God gave them the land of Canaan. 'The works of the Lord are great and studied by all who take delight in them.' One reason people study theology is that they have become people who take delight in what God has done. Yes indeed, says the psalm, the logical consequence is that you will want to study it. The Prayer Book version says that these works of God are 'sought out' by those who have pleasure in them, and that is the basic meaning of the verb. If you go looking for something you need, this is a word you could use. To study is to ask hard questions about something that matters.

Once again it is a plural word. The psalm is talking about a community matter. It presupposes the engagement of my whole mind, but it also presupposes that my study takes place in community. Over recent centuries higher education has become a rather individual matter. It is a process whereby I write my essays and take my exams so that I get my degree. In Jerusalem I have seen Jewish people studying torah together, and it is a very different activity. People sit in little groups, the whole person engaged, intent, fingers wagging, living out the conviction that studying scripture is a corporate enterprise and that a body is never more alive than when its members are studying scripture.

The psalm presupposes that people were enthusing over the great acts of God which made the people of God what they were. When did they do that? The commentators often reckon that a psalm like this belongs at a festival such as Passover or Tabernacles when Israel especially remembered the great acts of God, Israel's equivalent to Easter or Christmas. It was of the essence of those festivals that they were occasions when people gathered together and lived together as a community. That gives me the excuse to include a third feature of the nature of a community, the element of common life. In Britain in recent years it is extraordinary how the Greenbelt/Spring-Harvest phenomenon has brought the camping festival back into the life of the believing community. There is something special about time spent living with other Christians like that and focusing on the faith together.

There is something else about that celebrating of the great acts of God. It was not just a matter of recalling what God had done centuries ago. Those events were celebrated on the assumption that they were still having an effect now, that they had set going a process which was still under way, even that they had established a pattern that could still be repeated now. There may be a more explicit hint of this in that phrase 'I will praise the Lord with my whole heart.' The verb there is not the ordinary word for praise but the word you would usually use in giving thanks for something God had done for you personally. It is the word for giving your testimony. The celebrating relates to new events, not just old ones.

Community involves having your own experience of being rescued from oppression, sustained in the wilderness, committed to the covenant, and taken to the edge of the promised land. It implies not just individual experiences of that, but experiences of it that people share with each other. I once read a fascinating article about liturgy, justice, and tears, about bringing our own suffering and the suffering of others into worship. The psalms are very good at that, of course. The article talked about a service in South Africa during apartheid where people brought not only bread and wine to the communion table, but also a set of chains and a rubber bullet and a passbook. They brought their suffering into worship, into the very service which focuses on the suffering of the crucified God. That belonged to the essence of their life as a community. I have no doubt that it brought them together as a community. I have seen that happen myself when people have grieved before God over illness and death within the college.

It is usually difficult to do, for at least two reasons. One is the cost to the sufferer, for to talk about our suffering before God implies talking about it to ourselves, coming to terms with it. The other reason is related. It is theological. It is Job's friends' problem. We are not sure the faith can cope with it, whether it really has the answers, whether God really knows about suffering. With our heads we know that God does, but in our hurt hearts we are less certain and we are not sure we can risk opening the question. In a community we owe it to each other to enable each other to give voice to the grief, hurt, and pain of the people of God and of the world, and when we do that we will find we are a community in grief, a community in helpless prayer. We will then find that one way or another the God of the signs and wonders of the exodus, of the wilderness, and of the promised land will be our God. We will find we are a community in wonder at what God does in our midst, a community in answered prayer, a community in testimony which occupies the whole heart and mind.

There is one other feature of Israelite community life that I notice in Psalm 111. It is a community of obedience. They were a people who lived by Yahweh's precepts and knew that those precepts were a reliable guide for life (verse 7). They were a people who lived by the covenant which Yahweh had ordained for ever (verse 9). They knew that the fear of Yahweh, reverence before Yahweh, awe before Yahweh, obedience to Yahweh, was the key to wisdom, the key to understanding (verse 10). And only insofar as they were a community in obedience would all the other things be true. Their worship would not count for anything otherwise. Their study of God's acts would not count for anything; it would not lead to real wisdom, only to knowledge. Their common life would be imperilled if there was no obedience.

Obedience in what respect? Jesus once said that the heart of that torah which the psalm commits itself to was love for God and love for one's neighbour. When he was asked to explain it a bit more, he told a strange story about a man who got mugged and was ignored by the people who were committed to obedience but received neighbourly treatment from the source you would least expect. So the question is, what would it be like to be a community of obedience in love, a community which did not just sing about the servant king but itself comprised a servant community?

(ii)

On the occasion of Ann's seizure, one of the Bishops' Inspectors commented that it was bound to make a big difference to the college having the principal's wife taken off to hospital like that, and I was a bit surprised or puzzled. Perhaps it did, but the thing it made me think more about was whether the principal's wife having her illness rather made a difference to the college all the time. There would be a number of reasons why I would periodically think that I had no reason to be there because I was no good at the job (though that was not incompatible with believing that I could do the job at least as well as anyone else). One of them was that there were things I could not do because of Ann, ways in which being committed to Ann held me back or occupied my time or grieved my heart. But then I told myself that the other side to that coin, the positive aspect, was what Ann brought to college.

As well as contributing to my making, she contributed to the making of our students. I have this hunch that long after anything I have ever said about the Old Testament, about which I care so passionately, has disappeared from most people's memories, some aspect of the memory of Ann abides with them, and in some way they have been shaped by her, as I have been shaped and as our sons have been. As well as the shaping that comes about through relationships with particular individuals, I have the suspicion that she formed part of the identity of that community. The fact of having her as the principal's wife has determined something of its nature, and has even contributed significantly to its growth in health and maturity as she has shrunk.

The American theological ethicist Stanley Hauerwas has written among other things about Christian understandings of suffering and medicine and mental retardation. In a book called *Naming the Silences* (Clark, 1993; p. 2) Hauerwas asks what we mean by 'pointless suffering' and suggests it means that 'we cannot situate this life with its suffering in any ongoing story carried by a community that can make this suffering person's life its own'. That draws attention both to the deepest problem about Ann's illness and to the most positive aspect of its mystery. The deepest problem is that God achieves so much through that illness, perhaps much more than God achieves through my ministry, but that this achievement of God's comes about through a systematic ignoring of what seems best for Ann, through a systematic withdrawing of so much that she has valued, her work, her independence, her mobility, her intellectual ability, so that she is reduced to a person who sits in her chair unable to remember what day it is. And yet the edge is taken off the awfulness of that insofar as her life is situated and her story carried by this community which makes her life of loss its own and shares its love with her.

> Historically speaking, [Hauerwas goes on] Christians have not had a 'solution' to the problem of evil. Rather, they have had a community of care that has made it possible for them to absorb the destructive terror of evil that constantly threatens to destroy all human relations. (p. 53)

The community has shared its love with her, and has shared its love with me. I recall some years ago puzzling over Romans 5:5 for quite a long period, worrying at it like a dog with a bone. 'Hope does not disappoint or shame, because God's love has been poured into our hearts through the Holy Spirit who has been given to us.' What does that mean? Not, 'What do the words mean?' But, 'What reality are they referring to?' I wondered whether there was some charismatic outpouring of God's love that I had not had and might seek from God. And yet perhaps one reason I stopped fretting over the question was the fact that such an outpouring as I might long for sounded rather frothy and triumphalistic. Even if God had indeed overwhelmed me with an awareness of love, I cannot see how I could have fitted it in with how Ann was. I had no doubt of God's love for me and no difficulty about expressing my love for God, but felt experience of God had for me to be experience of felt mystery more than experience of felt love.

That changed over those weeks which followed Ann's seizure, when I came to feel overwhelmed by love in a way I never had been before, but in a way that recognized hurt rather than ignored it. In another book called *Suffering Presence* (Clark, 1988) Stanley Hauerwas suggests that no matter how sympathetic people may be when we suffer, 'no matter how much they may try to be with and comfort us, we know they do not want to experience our pain'; it is a difficulty heightened and prolonged by chronic illness which alienates sufferer and family from other people (p. 77). So we deny our pain and pretend, and thereby increase our loneliness

(p. 78). The comment provides a clue to the question of why Christian communities often hide their pain from each other. 'We know', says Hauerwas, that other people 'do not want to experience our pain'.

We think we know. Because what I find odd about his comment is that it is at the same time deeply illuminating and deeply wrong, sharply contradicted by my experience (by his, too, in practice, I discover from correspondence with him). It was precisely the pain I felt that made many college people reach out to me as well as to Ann after her seizure, and made others grieve the more because they could not think of a way of reaching out to me, short of bringing me college food when I had 'flu, which was a paradoxical form of showing love, I thought.

Some were people who reached out to me because of the love that God had put in their hearts, and that disproves Hauerwas's dictum one way. Others reached out to me with that love that God inspired and used because of a particular reason, because of the pain in their own hearts.

One earlier Thursday we had been praying for people in chapel, and a student who was going through a particular experience of pain went forward to ask people to pray, and I found myself not moving out to pray with him, but staying in my place, crying. A well-meaning brother came to pray with me and I had to explain that I did not think I was weeping for myself this time, but for that other student. That term I looked in the eyes of people who came to sit with me and saw their hurt which gave them access to mine, and it was often then that I felt overwhelmed by love, overwhelmed by the love of human beings, whose real fleshly human love it was, but who were also vehicles of the love of God. And I said one day through my own tears to someone else whose pain I knew and which I could at that very moment see in their eyes as they simultaneously hurt for me – I said that it was not fair that they should be there supporting me when they had that hurt in their own hearts, but even as I said it I knew it was nonsense, dangerous nonsense at that. I was trying to make their own hurt pointless. They were instinctively letting their own pain bear its terrible fruit in their capacity to love me.

And I thought, 'Well, at least, if God could not create a world from which grief was absent, at least God has created a world in which this grief bears fruit rather than returning to earth having borne nothing.' And the fact that the overwhelming of God's love took place through the tears of people's grief made it possible to bring together Romans 5 and the fact of pain, in a way that is actually true to Paul, for he himself brings suffering and love together.

But why bring God in? Was this not just human love, and none the worse for that? Why bring God in?

One evening I went to bed straight after eating my supper because I was miserable and I could not think of anything else to do. But unfortunately I was evidently getting a bit better from the 'flu and was not so tired and could not get to sleep, so I just lay there feeling more and more miserable. I longed to have someone to put their arms round me. I know I could have got up and gone to see someone and that they would have, but perhaps I had been thinking about whether this was all too exclusively human, about whether God was just an extra level of interpretation I was putting onto human caring (and risking dishonouring it in its humanity). I cried out to God, 'I know you care, but your arms cannot be felt as a human being's can'. And then it was as if there were physical arms around me, and I felt embraced by God personally as I have never felt before. And I could sleep the sleep of the cared for.

I realized that there had been a particular sort of embrace that I had valued and subconsciously sought over previous weeks; not the regular sort of hug when you stand man-to-man, but a kind of hug that involved someone standing over me and seeming bigger than me, so that their embrace shielded me from the world and the future and my anxieties and life's demands. At the end of the Blessing of Moses in Deuteronomy 33 is the promise that underneath are the everlasting arms, but at the beginning of the Song of Moses in Deuteronomy 32 is the promise that God is a mother hen fluttering over its young, and it is that sense of being covered and protected that I have so valued as people have incarnated the protecting love of God to me. I was reminded, too, of Ruth's plea to Boaz to 'cover her' with the wings of his garments, as it were, and of Bruce Springsteen's wonderful song 'Cover me'.

Oddly, as well as reassuring me that God was real and not just an interpretation of human love, that supernatural experience of God's embrace gave extra value to the human love. Usually God had been reaching me through other people, and now I had more conviction that it was God who was caring for me, but that usually God chose to do that through other people. Why?

I came to recognize that there were reasons for that which were peculiar to me and which related to what God wanted to do with me. I do not think that in life in general I deny my pain, but I recognized that I had subconsciously felt I had to live with it alone. Perhaps I had assumed that there was a grief in Ann's illness that was peculiar to me and that I had to live with that alone. I would do that in the evening, for instance, when she had gone to bed and I would sit writing 400-page books. And I am not sure that that is wrong (though it may be). But whether it is right or wrong, paradoxically, the experience of that bout of Ann's illness made me face my loneliness, which I think I had barely owned, by causing people to irrupt into it, and also made me ask whether I was as boring or unlikeable a person as I thought.

But there is also a general theological reason for God's choosing to reach out to us through each other, which is that love is sacramental. We are physical people, and the physical embrace we offer each other is a sacrament of the embrace of God. God can feed us spiritually without bread and wine, but bread and wine is the normal way, because we are fleshly people. God can embrace us directly and not use other people, but using other people is the normal way because we are fleshly people. And people who hugged me in such a way as to make me feel protected became sacraments of the protectiveness of God.

There were one or two interesting characteristics about the people who became sacraments to me like that. I have mentioned that many of them had their own hurt. They were also mostly people who were nearly half my age, which provided a laugh several times as nurses who assumed that some of those who had gone to see Ann were her daughters were roundly put in their place. It also reminds me of the way God delights to use the younger rather than the elder child in Genesis, and I wonder whether it models something of the turning upside-down of expectations that may be true of the gospel. It also reminded me of something I had failed to convince the college about during the previous year, that we had within that community the pastoral resources to care for each other. Partly for reasons to do with worldly assumptions about the nature of community and leadership which are mentioned in the introduction to this chapter, the college did not believe that, but it acted like it, and I suppose I would rather it disbelieved in theory but believed in practice than the other way round, like the first of the two sons in the parable in Matthew 21.

In the meeting between the Bishops' Inspectors and the college's governing body to which I referred in chapter 1, we fell into some discussion of the nature of community in a theological college in the 1990s. One of the Inspectors wondered aloud whether the loss of the old markers of a residential college – everybody in chapel morning and evening, everybody eating all their meals together, and so on – would eventually mean the loss of any sense of community. Two governors who were students twenty years ago responded with one voice and enabled me to see something which I had half-seen but not quite articulated to myself. The old markers of a residential college community disappeared a quarter of a century ago. If we had been living on the capital of the past, we would already have been bankrupt.

The reality of the college community, which was always recognized by people who came in from outside, whether for an hour or a day or a week or a month, was little to do with whether people were all on parade at particular moments (as is just as well, because we are an individualistic lot who make our own decisions about whether to be on parade for anything). It was a reality in lots of little groups, networks, twos and threes and fours, some of which I never knew existed till those painful few weeks. And it was a reality in the way in which those groups were not closed self-indulgent cliques but a criss-crossing network, so that college was more like a church than it had ever been. In fact it was modelling (the two governors argued in unison) a realistic, viable vision of community for parish life. And as the opposite of closed self-indulgent cliques, these groups were a network open to a man in need, not requiring him to force his way into them (for he lacked the confidence to do that) but on their own initiative opening their arms to him and daring him turn away. The church, says Hauerwas, is a company of people who have learned how to be ill and to ask for help and how to be present to one another in and out of pain (p. 80).

One of the students said to me one day that term, 'It isn't going to be the same again, you know,' and the words strangely upset me. It was partly because I was at that stage of 'flu when you get overwhelmed by waves of moroseness and gloom, but it was partly because they were strangely pregnant words, real prophetic words, words whose significance I have kept pondering. Did it mean, 'It wasn't going to be the same' for Ann physically – was she ever going to be the same? In fact she got nearer to that than I would have dreamt she would get. Did it mean 'it wasn't going to be the same' because once you have had that kind of experience you can never relax again? 'We may laugh again, but we will never be young again?' Certainly I could not contemplate jaunts with Ann half-way round the world to the Middle East or South Africa or somewhere any more (but here I am taking her to the USA!). And if Ann did get to being as mobile as she was before, what would be the point? Something like that seizure would happen again one day, or something else quite different, so what was the point of going through it and coping with it and recovering when you are going to have to go through it again in some other form?

Or did the words mean that the way people related to me would never be the same and that I would not be the same? One day I was saying to God that presumably now we get back to normal and I cease belonging to those networks of relationships and I have to stay alone again – things do become the same again. And I half-expected God to say, 'Don't be stupid,' because that is what God is often saying to me, but instead God said, 'Yes,' at which I was a bit taken aback. God did nuance the toughness of the 'Yes' by promising me that there would be people who would reach out to me and that I had to receive them for what they are and who they are and live with the insecurity of that.

It turns out that thirty or forty days in the wilderness and being ministered to by angels may be simultaneous experiences rather than sequential ones. In the wilderness itself God ministers to you through people in miraculous ways. Stone is turned into bread by the word which comes from the mouth of God. But by definition that is an experience that you have to let God stay in charge of. It is not even covenanted. You have to accept the angelic ministry as it comes in the form in which it comes, and live from day to day, from loaf to loaf, from hand reaching out to hand reaching out – and live through the times when there are no angels or loaves or hands. If being overwhelmed by love is the fruit of the Holy Spirit, then it is presumably bound to be a temporary rather than a permanent experience in this age, because that is the nature of the Holy Spirit's work. Jesus' experience repeats Job's in illustrating the way the Adversary sometimes has the power under God to take us into what looks like God-forsaken wildernesses. The Spirit gives us foretastes of what heaven is like, but they are foretastes, which in this age remain incomplete and are designed to provide guarantees and to provoke yearning. On the other hand you also have to be wary of failing to recognize angels and loaves and hands, insisting that all you see is stones when God is doing those miracles of provision for you – at least, I have to be wary of that. For it is true that 'hope does not disappoint or shame us, because God's love has been poured into our hearts by the Holy Spirit who has been given to us'.

6

Darkness

'Yahweh is my light and my salvation': so Psalm 27 begins. So, without Yahweh, apparently I lack light and salvation. What I experience is darkness and loss, gloom and calamity, night and disaster, autumn bringing winter and decline bringing death.

Someone was talking to me a year or two ago about the way gloom descended upon her as winter drew on, and about a suspicion that this mirrored the literal gloom of winter. Perhaps the darkness of winter makes it harder for us to escape the inner gloom of our own hearts.

A few weeks after Ann's seizure, when life was beginning to get back to normal, a friend asked whether it was time I talked out the implications of the experience for me personally, talked about the broader implications of coping with Ann's illness and how I felt about that. I had in fact wondered about that myself, so I surprised her with a positive response rather than chewing her head off about not wanting to indulge in that nonsense. I got in touch with a former student who is a hospital chaplain and has a counselling ministry, and went to see him half-a-dozen times. It was extremely useful, and some of the thoughts I have attempted to express in this book emerged in those sessions. That possibility that the darkness of winter makes it harder for us to escape the inner gloom of our own hearts reminds me now of something which happened in one of them.

On that occasion I cried when I was in the midst of articulating something that was actually positive and hopeful. This crying at an illogical moment had already happened once or twice, and I was quite angry about it, and I wanted to know why it happened. The counsellor was the type who would usually say nothing and turn the question back on me (which usually worked), but this time he responded. He suggested that articulating hope and facing darkness, gloom and pain were close to each other, because the hopeful statement was a denial of the gloom that I was inclined to feel. Joy and pain are next door to each other. Inside me there are dark corners where the gospel has not yet had its way, places where I do not really believe there is gospel, places where all is gloom and winter.

That in turn reminds me of a November Friday when as a college we sought to wait on God together, and people talked of the dying autumns of their own lives that mirrored the autumn of nature. And it was only November! 'How will we face January and February?' I asked myself. Sometimes January and February are tough times in college, as in churches, and one reason is that we cannot face the January and February, the gloom, despondency and darkness, in our own spirits. We repress them and they come out in ways that evade the pain but lose the potential for growth that they contain. It is with regard to these, among other things, that Psalm 27 invites me to say, Yahweh is my light and my salvation.

In that sharing in November I remember feeling downcast at the fact that for me the stripping of leaves seemed to be a perpetual experience, as if autumn never ends and spring never comes, but someone pointed out to me that this is where the illustration breaks down, because stripping in itself turns out to be fruit-bearing. Later I came across this quotation from John Donne, from a sermon on Christmas Day 1624 (no trivial sermons on Christmas Day in the seventeenth century!).

God hath made no decree to distinguish the seasons of his mercies; in paradise, the fruits were ripe the first minute, and in heaven it is always autumn, his mercies are ever in their maturity. We ask . . . our daily bread, and God never says you should have come yesterday, he never says, you must again tomorrow, but today if you will hear his voice, today he will hear you. If some king of the earth have so large an extent of dominion, in north and south, as that he hath winter and summer together in his dominions, much more hath God mercy and judgement together: he brought light out of darkness, not out of a lesser light; he can bring thy summer out of winter, though thou have no spring; though in the ways of fortune, or understanding, or conscience, thou have been benighted till now, wintered and frozen, clouded and eclipsed, damped and benumbed, smothered and stupefied till now, now God comes to thee, not as the dawning of the day, not as in the bud of the spring, but as the sun at noon to illustrate all shadows, as the sheaves in harvest, to fill all penuries. All occasions invite his mercies, and all times are his seasons.[1]

Donne did not know that in Israel itself you can move from snowy winter to desert sun within an hour (I dare say you can do the same in California).

That in turn reminds me of the English carol 'When the green blade riseth':

When our hearts are wintry, grieving, or in pain,
Thy touch can bring them back to life again.

'Yahweh is my light and my salvation. So whom shall I fear?', the psalm goes on. 'Of whom shall I be afraid?' In one sense I do not do fear. I do not get afraid. It's not a virtue or anything; I just have that bit missing, like embarrassment. Once on a college trip to Israel we were driving a minibus through a village near Hebron and people started throwing rocks at the vehicle. There seemed a chance that something very nasty would happen, and I was in the navigator's seat, in the front line for getting hurt if it did. I remember thinking, 'This is an interesting experience, but it will be good when we are out of here.' I also remember realizing afterwards that I had not exactly felt afraid, as some people had (one of my colleagues will probably never forgive me for that piece of mis-navigation).

---

[1] From *The Lord of the Journey* (ed. Roger Pooley and Philip Seddon; Collins, 1986) p. 67; reprinted from *The Sermons of John Donne*, 10 vols. (University of California Press, 1953–62), vol. 6, p. 172.

On the other hand I do get anxious, which is different, but related. I can worry, I can wish there was somewhere to hide, or that there was someone to hide me, to protect me.

And the psalm dares me to say, 'Yahweh is the stronghold of my life' or 'the refuge of my life; of whom shall I be afraid?'. There are women's refuges where the one thing you can be sure of is that there will be no men there, nobody to be the life-threatener that your husband or your lover or your pimp could otherwise be: a place where you can begin to learn to relax and regain the strength to face life.

Which takes us into seeking, for that is where it takes the psalmist in offering us this testimony. 'One thing have I asked of Yahweh, that will I seek after.' One of my colleagues once described someone else as a 'focused' person. It made me think about the idea of being focused, and about what it involves. I take it to mean something like this. You can be a person who does all sorts of things, but they are a bit like grapeshot. There is no unity to them, no one aim that holds them together. You do not concentrate on certain things because they matter. You are all over the place, easily distracted from one thing to another. That is key to the idea, I think. But lying behind it is the idea that there is no centre to what you are and do. There is no 'one thing'. (Admittedly one of my women colleagues commented that focusing on one thing was a men's luxury.)

I find it interesting that Psalm 27 comes to talk about this in the context of talking about darkness. It reminds me of John of the Cross, the person from whom we get the phrase 'the dark night of the soul'. John was an interesting person, a Spanish theologian and mystic in the sixteenth century. I had always thought of him as rather remote until I discovered that he had a job rather like mine. He was the principal of a community, trying to get a grip of the students and keep the church authorities happy and write the odd book and keep the adventurous women theologians as content as he could.

One piece of bad news I discovered is that in *The Dark Night* he talks about two dark nights of the soul. There is one which is self-imposed as well as the one which is God-imposed. It involves our committing ourselves to a life of denial in order to find the real light in God. Except that John talks about it as finding the real darkness in God. Because paradoxically, the light of God is so bright that when it really shines on us it blinds us, it puts us into darkness.

When John talks about the dark night, he talks about it in terms of a stripping away of the things that do not really matter to us. It takes us back to basics. It raises the question of who we really are and what we are really aiming at. You could argue that the question whether you prefer grapeshot or targeting is a Myers-Briggs sort of question, it is a personality question. You can indeed hit things with grapeshot, but it is usually reckoned to be wasteful. It does not achieve as much as targeting, as focusing. So John of the Cross sees it as a virtue that darkness, stripping, takes us back to basics, makes us concentrate on what deserves concentration. 'There is one thing I do: I am going for a target,' says Paul. 'There is one thing you lack,' says Jesus to a young man with a lot of possessions. 'There is only one thing that is needed,' he says to a woman worrying about the dinner. 'There is one thing I know: I can see now,' says the man born blind. 'There is one thing I have asked of Yahweh', says the psalm, 'one thing'.

If we are in the dark at the moment, or if we find ourselves walking in the dark in due course, John says, we need to let it strip us, let it focus us, let it make us handle the question of what really matters, what we really want. It raises the question of whether we have a target, whether we are over-preoccupied by things we have got or things we have to do, whether we know the one thing that is of key importance to who we are and what we are about. It raises the question whether we are focused. The psalm's focus bears consideration. 'One thing I have asked from Yahweh, that is the thing I am seeking, the thing I am insisting on. It is to dwell in Yahweh's house all the days of my life, to see Yahweh's beauty, and to inquire in Yahweh's palace.'

Yahweh's house, Yahweh's beauty, Yahweh's palace, sound a fair focus. It is just the thing that John of the Cross wants us to focus on. When he pictures us deliberately imposing darkness on ourselves he talks about us needing to be inclined not to the easiest but to the most difficult, not to the most delightful but to the harshest, not to the most gratifying but to the less pleasant, not to what means rest but to hard work, not to the consoling but to the unconsoling. . . .

To come to the pleasure you have not, you must go by a way you enjoy not; to come to the knowledge you have not, you must go by a way in which you know not; to come to the possession you have not, you must go by a way in which you possess not; to come to be what you are not, you must go by a way in which you are not.

It is terribly negative, but it is to give us a focus, to strip us down, but to strip us down to what matters. It invites us to 'one thing'.

We are free not to volunteer for that self-imposed darkness. But if the other darkness comes to us, it imposes itself. It is a common feature of training for ministry. People give up the focus they had before and they are on the way to another focus, but while they are training they are in between. They may take to training like a duck to water, but they may hate it, and they may then lash out at the church and the college and the universities and – if they dare – at God. When they do the last, lash out at God, then they are getting somewhere. They and God are doing serious business because they are in the dark and God put them there, and the question is what is God going to do about it. And the answer is usually, 'Nothing for a while', because quick salvation would short-circuit the process and rid them of the chance to discover who they are in this uncomfortable place with yesterday's focus taken away.

They are still free in relation to this darkness. They do not have to co-operate. God does not abandon them because they resist it. It will come to an end, and beginning some new ministry will give them a new focus, give them relief and a form of light, an escape from a darkness. But it will be a cheap escape, and the new focus will not be the psalm's focus. 'One thing have I asked from Yahweh. That will I seek after.' To serve God? To be ordained? 'One thing have I asked from Yahweh, that will I seek after: that I may dwell in the house of Yahweh all the days of my life, to see the beauty of Yahweh and to inquire in Yahweh's temple.' That is the 'one thing' that is worth going for.

There are three facts about God there. Yahweh has a house, Yahweh has beauty, and Yahweh has a palace. Yahweh's having a house to live in reflects the fact that Yahweh is a person, just like Yahweh's having a temper to lose. Admittedly rather than having a proper, permanent, fixed, stone-built dwelling-house, Yahweh preferred a tent. This preference for camping is the aspect of the doctrine of God which I have always found most difficult to understand. But whether it was a tent or a house it meant that Yahweh was a person like us and you could go up to this dwelling-place and walk in and see Yahweh.

Yahweh has beauty. I have puzzled about that because it does not obviously fit with the rest of Psalm 27. This is not a soppy psalm, full of the equivalent to 'Jesus how lovely you are'. It is a gritty, robust, determined psalm, one which presupposes that Yahweh is a gritty, robust, determined kind of God. But it believes in the grace, the goodness, and the attractiveness of Yahweh, and those features are expressed in Yahweh's being a gritty, robust, determined kind of God. Which fits with Yahweh having a palace, a rather splendid kind of house. Hebrew does not have a word for 'temple' and uses the word used in other contexts for 'palace', so that when the word 'temple' occurs in the Old Testament it is usually a word which reminds us that Yahweh is like a monarch with all the power and privilege of monarchy in the ancient world. Yahweh lives in a palace; but the door is open and we can walk in and talk to the sovereign. 'I have a personal, powerful God with all the attractiveness of that', says the psalm. 'The one thing that I have asked, the one thing that I am seeking, is to live with that person, to ask that sovereign for things, to thrill at that robust and gritty God who is committed to me, who takes a "one thing" attitude to me as if I was the only person in the world, because this God is magically able to do that with me and with each of my brothers and sisters.'

And so I will walk through the darkness because there is light on the other side. 'Yahweh will hide me in his shelter in the day of trouble, conceal me in the shadow of his tent, set me high upon a rock. Now he will lift up my head above my enemies round about me, and I will offer sacrifices in his tent with shouts of joy. I will sing and make melody to Yahweh.'

The reference to Yahweh's 'tent' is noteworthy. The psalm knows that Yahweh is still an incurable backpacker, even after the temple is built, always on the move, on to the next place, ahead of you or with you or following you, but never settling down. I will be there in God's dwelling, in God's company, eating and drinking and laughing with God. My ambition will be realized. There is that one thing I want, one thing I have focused on, and I am focusing on it the more because of the pressure of darkness. That is the nature of the experience if you let it have its way. It will produce the goods. The stripping down to one thing means focusing on that one thing and reaching it, because the one who drives into darkness really is light and salvation.

When you are walking through the dark night, it is no use for someone else to tell you that it will come to an end. You have to say it to yourself, you have to be able to give assent to it for yourself. That is partly why John of the Cross wrote his books. He wanted you to read his account of how people come through the dark night and at least to know that you are not the first person to walk that way. That is what Psalm 27 wants. It does not mean that this stops being real darkness. It means you may be able to believe that darkness is not all there is, able to imagine finding that 'Yahweh is my light and my salvation'.

7

Friendship

For Ann and me, as for many people, a period in our mid-twenties saw several major changes happen over quite a short period. Over a year or two or three, we ceased to be students, started work, got married, settled in an area where we had never lived before, and started a family. Whereas both of us had previously had a group of friends, mostly of our own sex, these five events worked together to produce the very different situation that we were not only each other's best friend but more or less each other's only friend. We could not keep up the old friendships in the same way, and events conspired against our making many new ones. It did not seem to be a problem; indeed I did not realize that it was happening.

In a strange way, it has been Ann's illness that has changed all that. Over the period of years since Ann had to give up work a number of people have reached into her life and become friends to her. It has been a mutual business; they are not merely people offering support to her and me. Over the more recent period since Ann's seizure I have had the experience of a number of people elbowing their way into my life, as I think of it, more forcibly than people needed to do with Ann. It has made me aware of the friend-shaped blank that had been there for a while for both of us – because I doubt if God's design was for two people to be everything to each other. For me, they have been people who came to make me believe that I was loved, people who asked questions that made me think new thoughts, and of course people who enabled me to stand when I might have fallen over.

So what is a friend? I suppose I am talking about someone you appreciate, someone you enjoy spending time with, someone you are especially glad to see, someone interesting. But of course there is more to it than that. It is someone you have come to trust, someone you have come to commit yourself to in some way. It is someone with whom you find yourself sharing who you are, sharing things you might not share with everyone. It is someone you find you want to do things for, give things to, when you know what they like. In Hebrew and Greek two of the common words for 'friend' are related to words for 'love', and that tells you something about friendship. It is a form of love. And in Hebrew and in Greek, 'love' is a matter of mind, and feelings, and action. You love God with mind and feelings and action, says Deuteronomy, because that is what love is like. Of course our love is a reflection of God's. God loves with mind, and feelings, and action. God appreciates us, enjoys spending time with us, is glad to see us, finds us interesting, trusts us, make a commitment to us, shares intimate secrets with us.

And all that applies to human relations. So when you love your neighbour as another human being like yourself, this love, too, is a matter of mind, and feelings, and action, like God's love for us and ours for God. And like love between us and God, of course, it is of the essence that this is two-way. It would not work if only one of two people wanted that kind of friendship.

Again God's friendship with us may be like our love for God in that it tends to develop gradually. We do not find that the whole of God is forced on us at once, and we do not give all of ourselves to God at once, even if there are moments when we take whole leaps forward in our awareness of being loved by God and in our loving of God. This, too, is true of human friendship. It comes about gradually, and it does so because both parties subconsciously take the risk of letting it happen, stage by stage.

There is indeed risk. God takes risks in entrusting intimate secrets to us, in sharing the ministry of the Godhead in the world with us, instead of just getting on with it. We take risks with God in opening up our lives to heavenly scrutiny and looking at ourselves through God's eyes and saying we will do what God wants and go where God wants us to go. We take risks in sharing our inner secrets with each other, too, the risk of looking stupid and sinful and proud and narrow to the other person, and thus to ourselves.

Friendship takes time and energy too. That is why there are limits to the number of friends you can have, and why a married couple may find themselves making fewer friends than they did when they were single. We have noted the wonderful fact that God has infinite capacity to share with an infinite number of beings, with each of us. But we are not God and we do not have the resources to share with everyone.

So what is the point of taking the risk and expending the energy? Why not hide from other people, as some people do? And why should friendship be the subject of Christian reflection? One reason is the way our friends change us. As in marriage, which is a form of friendship if you are lucky, our friends may decide that they themselves want to change us, and they may succeed in some ways, though these changes may be a bit external. If you could see me, you might think that that my clothes are garish: people say I will have an identity crisis in California because I will be just like everyone else. But you should have seen me before one or two of my colleagues started working on me. They are still working on my driving; usually the best I can do is sit in the back seat and let someone else do it.

The more profound changes come about when people are not trying. Some of them come about because we like something about a friend. It is one of the things that we appreciate about them and we find ourselves thinking the same way as they do. They have changed us. Or maybe we think, 'Well, if they reckon that thing is important or interesting or worthwhile, perhaps there is something in it, or at least I would like to find out about it and understand it because it is part of them.' Or we think, 'That is off the wall, how can someone possibly think like that?' And if it were anyone else, we would dismiss it, but because it is a friend we do not dismiss it. We want to understand, because we love this other person. And we find that the thing that seemed off the wall is not so crazy after all when looked at through the prism of this other personality. And so we may end up changing our thinking, and our attitudes, and our lives, and therefore our ministries. That is what friendship can do.

There is also a reverse process, because all this is mutual if you are friends. You yourself are off the wall in some ways. I know I am, because my colleagues have told me. (I looked up the expression in a dictionary and it said 'crazy', so I looked it up in a different dictionary and it just said 'unconventional', which I found more acceptable, so I bought that dictionary.) I find that a friend will ask me why I think in a certain way, or act in a certain way, and I have to work it out and say it in a way I have not before. And by that process friends help you discover things about yourself.

You probably do that in the process of saying things that may look stupid or sinful or proud or narrow. But more often than not in my experience, your friend does not think you are stupid (in fact probably tells you that you are stupid for thinking you are stupid) and is not appalled by the skeletons in your cupboard. From time to time I have had the experience of a friend telling me apologetically that something I had tried to do which was meant to be nice or helpful for them, actually worked the opposite way because of something else about them which I could not allow for, and they were very apologetic and felt bad about themselves. In contrast, I was amused and was given an odd kind of pleasure because they had had to show me something about themselves which they felt a bit sheepish about, but to me was just another bit of the jigsaw of this person whom I loved. One of my friends often used to say, 'Do not laugh at me' when I grinned at something she shared with me, but my smile was a smile of delight that I had discovered a bit more of her.

Of course the things you discover about yourself through your friendships may be things you do not like, and you may feel you want to change them. If you are really unlucky and have fallen into really bad friendships, as it were, your friend may not let you off the hook. One of the friendships I have most valued was like that. This friend would make the most outrageous, demanding observations about how I lived my life and how I ought to live it and how I thought about things and how I ought to think about them and how I saw myself and how I ought to see myself, and I could not ignore these observations because they came out of love, and they risked changing me; indeed they did change me. In its way this chapter and maybe every chapter in this book is the fruit of friendship. Your friends change you and therefore they change your ministries.

That is the upside of friendship. There are two aspects of the downside that occur to me. I have already hinted at one. There can be a sadness about making friends in some circumstances because they are likely to be of limited shelf-life. Most friendships, even the deep ones, have a short sell-by date. The single toughest aspect of our move from Britain to America is the effective cutting of ties with friends.

It is our own experience of something we see people at college go through each year. On the last day of the college year in June we distribute the 'Ember List', a leaflet containing the leavers' photographs and details of where they are going, so that people can pray for them. It includes some biographical data which people write themselves, and one of the things that people often comment on is the importance of the friendships they made at college, the people they got to know. That same day is also the day when everyone is saying goodbye, and a good few tears are shed. So the last day of the year brings out the upside and the downside of the fact that the friendships that people make are among the most important things of their time at college.

One person said to me one year in some anguish, 'Why does God always take people away?' Here she was moving to a parish in a part of the country where she had never lived before, and having once more to start again. She had had to leave the people she loved in her home town to go to the place where she had spent most of her working life before college, then she had had to leave the people she loved there to come to college, now she had to leave the people she loved in college. You may be able to keep up one or two friendships by occasional visits and you can talk to people on the phone but many of the friendships cannot carry on growing in the way they could before.

A few weeks after the leavers service one year, Ann and I had lunch with a couple to whom we had got close and who had left that summer, and it was lovely to be able to do that, but I found myself feeling sad even while I was there. I realized that this reunion was reminding me that actually we would hardly ever see this couple compared with the way things had been when we saw them nearly every day. Meetings like that are more reminders of something that had once been than a growing development of something.

It can be worse. A few years ago we had an Australian couple in college as tutors for a year. When they went back to Australia, one was even more aware of that sadness because they were not just going to Liverpool or Exeter where in theory one could still see them. As far as we knew we would never see each other again till heaven. (The irony is that they have actually been to Britain several times since.)

What seems to me to happen is that our friends become part of us and we of them. One reason is the process of mutual influence which I have described. When the friendship has effectively to cease for geographical or other reasons, it is thus like the separating of Siamese twins. As Ann and I are in the midst of saying goodbyes, I have found myself often singing the line from a Paul Young song, 'Every time you go away you take a little part of me.' In the song the phrase applies to romantic love; it seems to me to apply to friendship. The same is true of Ella Fitzgerald's classic 'Every time we say goodbye, I die a little' (never mind about Mick Hucknall).

There is another aspect to the poignancy of all this. When you get to know someone, one of the paradoxical results is that the more you know, the more you realize there is to know. I suppose the converse must be true. The more you let yourself be known, the more mystery there is about you which your friend has seen the corner of and got into dialogue with you about, and therefore the more there is that you might learn about yourself and the more you might be able to grow for God's sake if this friendship continued. Then in that form it has to end.

In John 15 Jesus talks about God pruning us, and I can only think that separating from friends, losing them in this sense, is part of the pruning process that is involved in life itself. It is therefore itself something that can make us grow. Things are taken away not because there is no growth and not to prevent growth but because there is growth and to encourage more growth. Outside their kitchen window the couple I just referred to had some tomato plants that they had inherited from their cottage's previous occupant. The plants had lovely yellow flowers and some little green tomatoes, and our friends did not know that in order to grow any proper tomatoes in our climate, you have to stop the pretty yellow flowers growing after the fourth branch. When God takes away, or when life takes away or the system takes away, God can make that the means of more fruit-bearing, not less. This does not take away the sadness involved in the ending of friendships, or the ending of one stage in friendships, but it may take the edge off the sadness. It means it is worth facing the cost for the sake of what we give each other and what we gain.

There is another downside involved in making friends, a different risk from the one I mentioned earlier. It is a risk that headlines in the newspapers periodically make us aware of, the risk that friendship love can turn into falling in love. I do not know any watertight ways of ensuring that this does not happen. Now, for people who are in a position to fall in love, that may be fine, and no doubt falling in love with a friend is a better idea than trying to make friends with someone you have fallen in love with. There are guidelines for pastoral relationships that can help one avoid the particular forms of risk in those relationships, but the same issues arise in friendships. And it could be that the risks will frighten us about friendships and about pastoring. As with the physical dangers of ministry in the inner city, such as the danger of being mugged, there is no way of eliminating risk.

When Harry Met Sally is my all-time number three film (behind *Paris, Texas* and *Once Upon a Time in America*, if you must know, with *Leaving Las Vegas* recently reaching number 4: you see, I have dark tastes, and *When Harry Met Sally* only tests the rule, because Harry has such a dark side; I suppose *Casablanca* comes next). But on a good day, what I now feel about *When Harry Met Sally* is the same as I do about that Hauerwas remark in Chapter 5, that it is deeply illuminating (and a whole lot of fun) but actually wrong. Its theme is that men and women can never be friends, because sex will always get in the way. Even if it does not for the woman, it will for the man, and that is enough. I have long viewed that as a deeply sad but true thesis, but I have felt myself challenged to rethink it.

This started with another American piece of pastoral theology, a book called *Sexuality and Spirituality* edited by James Nelson, that argued among other things for the possibility of friendships that were sexual without being genital. It talked about that with regard to same-sex friendships between gay people, but also with regard to cross-sex friendships between heterosexual people. I had long assumed that such friendships were bound to be neither one thing nor the other – they were bound to be frustrated, incomplete relationships, all foreplay (as it were). The vision Nelson offers is that there is such a thing as cross-sex friendship which recognizes and rejoices in the sexual nature of the relationship but which is not just an unnaturally foreshortened version of an affair. It is not frustrated because the two people do not end up in bed. It is a fulfilled version of something in its own right, not a frustrated version of something else.

This is a dangerous thesis. We live in a generation in which many marriages fall apart and in which many people have affairs, and that is true of Christians and it is true of clergy. In any congregation or among any group of clergy there will thus be a significant number who will have affairs one day, and a significant number whose marriages will break down. I do not believe it is possible to predict which it will be, nor possible for any of us to be sure 'It will not be me'.

That is frightening, but objectively it may be even more likely to affect us if we do not acknowledge it. Learning to have true, deep, sexual friendships might make us more likely to end up having an affair, but might have the opposite effect, particularly if we know what we are doing and avoid either demonizing sexual relationships or romanticizing them. They are a resource for us as human beings, and that is true in overlapping ways for people who suspect they are single for life, for people who hope that they are not, for the happily married, for the unhappily married, for heterosexual people and for gay people. They are a resource for us as human beings, and they are therefore a resource for us in ministry.

Sex is making it more and more dangerous to be involved in ministry with other people. That is obviously the case with heterosexual people, but you do not necessarily solve anything by avoiding ministry to people of the opposite sex, because you may just end up being tempted, misunderstood, seduced, or accused homosexually. The creative spark that there is in personal relationships, including their sexual element, is a resource for ministry.

There are things we can do to reduce the risk. As we can try to minister in threes rather than one-to-one, so we can look for our friendships to be inclusive not exclusive. We can talk with someone like a spiritual director about our friendships. We can look for the signs that suggest falling in love rather than friendship, and be prepared to act on what we find. I suspect that this is the biggest thing, for our culture of course assumes that if it is love it must be right, and we are subject to the temptation to think the same thing.

But if we decide that friendship is too dangerous to be risked, in general I think the risk of loss will be greater than the risk we avoid. The reasons again lie in the fruitfulness of friendship that I have tried to describe. That pruning on God's part can carve space into our lives and take us away from our idols and remove us to a foreign country to enlarge our understanding of God and enable us to discover who we are. Although I did once grow tomatoes, I know virtually nothing else about gardening, but I did once discover something about vines. We were driving through the Vale of Hebron in the West Bank, where some of the best vines grow. It was the first time I had visited the country in the spring and I had never seen vines in their pruned state. They are a terrible sight. Six months previously they would have been flourishing plants that had grown so extravagantly that they curled like a bower over your head and you could have reached up and let the fresh grapes fall into your mouth. Now they had been cut down so that they were nothing more than a black gnarled stump a foot or two high. We cannot have grapes without being willing to be a vine. We cannot be a vine without being willing to be pruned. We cannot have more grapes next year without being willing to be pruned. But we can grow grapes this year, and our friends will help us.

8

Hope

(i) Not the end of the story

Imagine that a tourism tycoon announces a competition for the designing of a new hotel in Sarajevo or Belfast or Freetown or wherever happens to be off-limits as a holiday destination when you read this. Imagine that she gives an award to a wondrous plan for an eight-storey complex with restaurants, jacuzzis, saunas, discos and swimming pools. Not only so, but she sends the plans out to tender and gives the contract to the construction company she fancies.

One day in the 580s BC, Jeremiah the prophet from Anathoth contracted to buy some land in circumstances that were about as absurd (see Jeremiah 32). For the second time in a decade Judah is under invasion from the Babylonians for wanting to run its own life, and Jerusalem is under siege. Jeremiah himself is in prison in Jerusalem. He has been going about declaring that the city will again fall to the Babylonians and that the best thing to do is surrender. This understandably displeases the political authorities, who view Jeremiah as a collaborator, a traitor, and a danger to community morale.

Things are evidently little better for Jeremiah's family. Their village lies a few kilometres north of Jerusalem, across the crucial line that divides northern Israel from southern Judah (as today the same village of Anata stands on the boundary of Jerusalem and the West Bank). Where Jeremiah came from will no doubt be another reason for the Jerusalem authorities' deep suspicion of him. He is, after all, not actually one of us.

One can guess that having the Babylonian army camped on your doorstep as it besieges Jerusalem does nothing for the quality of life in Anathoth. Perhaps it was one of the factors that led to the arrival of Jeremiah's cousin Hanamel to see if Jeremiah wanted to buy a piece of land from him. When things are bad, what people often have to do is realize their assets. That might mean selling your animals; in due course it might mean selling yourself and/or members of your family into slavery for a while. In between, it might mean selling some or all of your land (technically, leasing it). But you could not sell your land to just anyone. The land had been allocated by God to the tribes and families of Israel, and it had to stay in the family. You had to see if any of your relatives could and would buy it. So Hanamel came to pay a prison visit to Jeremiah, not out of concern for the prisoner's welfare but out of concern for his own.

Whether we think of the city of Jerusalem or the people of Judah and Israel, or the personal circumstances of Jeremiah or Hanamel, what we find is reason for gloom or anxiety at best, despair and hopelessness at worst. It may resonate with the gloom, anxiety, despair, and hopelessness that we all know. In many of the big traditional denominations in Britain there is reason enough for such gloom as they contemplate reduced congregations and economic difficulties. In individual churches, outward flourishing can sometimes conceal deep divisions or persistent inward-lookingness which has become the despair of their leadership. The jobs of individual Christians may cause them deep anxieties, whether they work in some part of the health service, the school system, higher education, or in business or industry with their ever-increasing demands and pressures – or if they have no job at all. In the dark hours of the night their personal lives may bring them near hopelessness as they ask themselves whether their marriages are in terminal decline or how on earth they can handle or help their children.

In a context of gloom, anxiety, hopelessness and despair, at community and individual levels, Jeremiah puts his shekels on the table and buys the piece of land from Hanamel. I wonder whether Hanamel could hardly believe his luck, whether he danced back to Anathoth laughing at the foolishness of the unworldly-wise prophet in buying land at this perilous moment in history. Is Jeremiah one tribe short of a chosen people, one candle short of a menorah? Why did he do it?

He did it because God told him to. Sometimes we do have the experience of knowing that God is pointing us in some direction which seems risky or stupid, and is looking to see how we respond. When some denominations are having a hard time paying their clergy (or even paying for their training) there are still people who are resigning jobs that they like because they believe God is telling them to train for full-time Christian ministry. Humanly it looks a stupid decision.

Afterwards, Jeremiah learned more; God told him something of what lay behind the revelation that Hanamel was coming and the instruction that Jeremiah was to say yes. It is often the case that only afterwards do we see why God looked for a particular step or allowed a particular thing to happen. In Jeremiah's case, it was a sign that the invasion of the land and the siege of the city by the Babylonians were not the end of the story. One day fields and vineyards would again be worth selling here. God had not finished with the city of Jerusalem and with the people of Judah and Benjamin and with individual people like Jeremiah and Hanamel. God still has their destiny in mind.

Why? How do we know? In part because this is not only not the end of the story; it is not the beginning of the story. Jeremiah knows that. After signing the contract he offers God a prayer which seems to read more like a history lesson. He summarizes how God created the world, delivered Israel from Egypt, gave them their land, and how this story now seems to be running into the sands of Babylonian occupation and transportation. There is some irony about the fact that Jeremiah himself does not seem quite to see the point of his own story. As is often the case, his very question contains the seeds of its own answer. How can God let this story run into the sand? Of course God cannot. The burden of the promises of the prophets of the exile is that the promises of God that go back to Abraham still apply. All they need is restating. Arguably that is all these prophets do.

The hope of Jerusalem, Judah, Benjamin, Jeremiah, and Hanamel is the hope of a story and a divine commitment that go back to Abraham.

The hope of the church and of the individual Christian believer lies in the same realities, the same story and the same commitment, now underlined by what God has done in Jesus. Might the church die out? Denominations may die out – existing, 'old' denominations, and 'new' ones that now seem vibrant and full of life. Patterns of ministry may change. Congregations may grow and shrink. Jobs may change. Yes, marriages may break down, parents make terrible mistakes, and children turn their backs on them. All these things may indeed be happening before our eyes. But they have written over them the promise 'Houses, fields and vineyards will again be bought in this land'. As the church we are entitled to be certain that God is committed to us, for the church itself is the fruit of that original unbreakable commitment to Abraham. As individuals we are entitled to the certainty that God is working out a purpose for us, that the promise embraces us.

Yes, says God, this city is to be given into the hands of the Babylonians. And when that happens, it will be nasty. The king, for instance, will be blinded as an act of sadistic punishment before he is taken off to Babylon itself, and as another act of sadistic punishment the last sight his eyes will see, the last image Zedekiah will take with him to Babylon, is the sight of his two sons being killed before him. But all this will not be the end. After that, 'I will surely gather them from all the lands where I banish them. . . . I will bring them back to this place and I will let them live in safety. They will be my people, and I will be their God. . . . I will rejoice in doing them good and I will assuredly plant them in this land with all my heart and soul' (Jeremiah 32:37–41).

It's not over till it's over. The moments of justified anxiety, gloom, hopelessness and despair stand under the promise of God. We may not be able to see how God can bring fruitfulness from them until afterwards, but we can believe that God will.

(ii) Soaking and hoping

Hoping is a familiar biblical and theological theme. Soaking is one I have just invented.

I once took part in a Holy Week retreat. It involved me in more church services than any other week of my life and in reading through the gospel story in every possible version and through most of the sections of the epistles that expound the significance of Jesus' passion and through most of the psalms that you could have imagined on Jesus' lips in the last days of his life, ones which illumine his experience. Towards the end of that week I felt as if I had been enveloped, soaked, immersed in the passion story in a more powerful way than I ever remembered. No matter what else I did that week when I was not in one of those services, I could not get away from the passion story. In one way it was a bit confusing because I found myself at midday having to read a section of Luke's Gospel which related to events which took place earlier than the section of Mark's Gospel which we had read earlier that morning, but in a strange way that heightened the soaking effect of living in the passion story for a week.

We inevitably live our lives in the world and in the church not by the passion story but by the values and the story of the world and of our own experience. And what we mostly need in our Christian lives is not some new truth which no one has told us yet but the old truth coming home to us afresh month by month and year by year and decade by decade. It is the thing that will then shape our thinking and shape our lives. We need to be immersed in that counter-story, that story which opposes the world's story.

It so happened that after celebrating the resurrection at the dawning of Easter Sunday, I then flew to Israel. On Easter Monday morning I was sitting in my favourite place in all the world, the terrace of the YMCA guest house, Peniel-by-Galilee, looking over the lake. I began to do something I had often told students to do but had never done myself, reading through the Galilee half of Mark's Gospel sitting in that place where you can actually see Capernaum, Bethsaida, Chorazim, and some other places that are traditionally associated with events in Jesus' life, and soaking myself in the pre-passion story, visualizing it unfolding before my eyes. But it was also Easter Week, and I continued working through the day-by-day lectionary readings, quite a lot of which focus on Galilee: 'Get up to Galilee,' Jesus says as soon as he is risen, and near Lake Galilee Jesus asks Peter those questions about love and commissions him. At the same time the lectionary had us reading through 1 Peter with its beginning which asserts that Jesus' resurrection rebirths us to a living hope.

For me that was the link between soaking and hoping. That soaking in the reality of the story of Jesus as the one who lived and taught and exercised that ministry there, and died and rose for me, reminded me of the basis for living hope. The soaking was key to the hoping. If I was to be a person of hope, it was on the basis of that story and of my being soaked in it.

It happened at a time I needed it. I had been going through a frustrating period of my life, not succeeding in completing a project I wanted to finish, and I had become clinically depressed. As it happened I had attended some lectures on pastoral theology, lectures on 'Hoping and Wishing'. The lecturer referred quite often to 'hopelessness', and I realized that each time he said the word it hurt me in the guts. I realized that my having got depressed and my hopelessness were related. One does get depressed or hopeless about particular things from time to time, but they can trip you into general hopelessness; that was what had happened to me.

But I also realized that you can only let yourself become aware of the reality of hopelessness, of the reasons for it, when you have realized that there are reasons for hope. It is unwise to think about hoping until you know there is a basis for it. It is difficult to face up to hopelessness until you know there might be an answer to it, a way of facing it.

I once said to Ann, 'Would you like a cream cake with your cup of tea?' She replied 'Have you got one?' She was wise. She did not wish to be conned into playing with the idea of a cream cake if I was about to reply, 'Tough, I forget to buy any.' First discover if there is something to hope for, then hope for it.

The good news of the gospel is that the God and Father of our Lord Jesus Christ has given us a new birth to a living hope through the resurrection of Jesus Christ from the dead. We hide from our hopelessness. But there are grounds for hope, and therefore it can be faced.

Isaiah 25 promises a day when the veil of mourning is taken away from everyone and God wipes away the tears from everyone's eyes and takes away the reproach of the people of God. God promises to handle our individual pains and griefs, and the reproach of the people of God which is also so depressing.

We are invited to name our hopelessnesses, about our own lives and about the church and about the world, because the resurrection of Jesus makes it possible to take the risk of doing that. It is the guarantee that there is hope in all these areas. That does not resolve the dialectic between glory and pain. Indeed in coming because of the resurrection to face hopelessness, we are taken back into the pain of the cross. But at least it does not leave us living with nothing, with unacknowledged pain.

We are invited to name our hopelessnesses and to let ourselves be soaked, enfolded, immersed in the counter-story of Jesus' life, death, and resurrection, because they are the basis for hope.

(iii) L'Arche

Just north of Paris at Trosly-Breuil is the original home of the l'Arche community, which brings together disabled and ordinary people to share their lives. One weekend Ann and I were there for a gathering of twenty professors, bishops, and other mortals from France, Belgium, Canada and Britain to discuss the theology of disability – or rather, as the invitation put it, 'to discuss how Jesus touches us in and through the poor, the broken, and the weak' – in the light of our own experience. The programme consisted chiefly of our simply sharing our 'testimonies'.

I have referred already to the ministry Ann exercises within college and elsewhere. When I go off to speak at some conference, often the thing people take away is not anything I have said but their meeting with Ann, though they rarely articulate what it is that has affected them. My guess is that she embodies human characteristics which belong to us all but which we normally seek to evade, such as fragility, dependence, and uncertainty. She brings these demons out into the open in such a way that they cease to be demons. Indeed, she reveals that they are angels. They are part of being human, part of the nakedness which humanity originally wore without shame, and they are therefore part of imaging God. Disabled people in their fragility, dependence and uncertainty embody the other side of that image. Ann then affirms the presence of God with her in her disability.

Disability through an illness like multiple sclerosis is not the same as the usually lifelong disability of the handicapped members of l'Arche, but it raises overlapping human and theological questions, as well as some questions of its own. The woman I married was not fragile, dependent and uncertain, but a person of independence, initiative, drive and energy who kept lots of balls in the air and in some respects behaved like a feminist before such were invented. I have been married to two personalities within the same body, yet to one human being. This must relativize the importance of 'personality' in the sense that the notion is so important to us and must point to a less self-contained basis for understanding the intrinsically human.

One consistent feature of Ann is the web of relationships in which she has been involved with family and friends. As the original Genesis 1 statement about the creation of humanity implies, being human is being in relationship with other people – such as the disabled. They smile, and therefore we are. Our essential humanity and value lie in being in such relationships of receiving and giving. This is true for disabled and ordinary alike, but the former may unveil the fact.

Another feature is the continuous story which Ann has lived. The story bridges that change in who she is and it is destined to continue towards those transforming changes that will embrace us all. It must be, then, that such changes do not threaten what authentic humanity means. Everyone has a story, even (especially?) the most disabled, the most poor, the most unpleasant, and the most wicked, and it is often their stories which are the most worth hearing and the most illuminating.

Another consistent feature of Ann is the physical body itself, recognizably one for all the change that has come about because of those wretchedly sclerosed myelin sheathes that prevent messages passing between brain and limbs. It draws attention to the important physical base to human personality. 'L'Arche is founded upon the body', Jean Vanier has written. It cannot be dualist. It involves 'a communication where body language is an essential component'.

Part of the philosophy of l'Arche itself is that the relationship between the disabled and the ordinary is two-way. Each gains from the other. People who work in l'Arche communities speak movingly of the ministry the disabled exercise to them. 'Every person, even the most handicapped, is called to be a source of grace and of peace for the whole community, for the Church and for humanity', declares the related 'Faith and Light' movement, which brings together families with disabled people for sharing, fiesta, celebration and prayer. And when it comes to celebration, says the Faith and Light charter, the handicapped are often less disabled than others because they are not imprisoned by convention, worried about efficiency, or fearful of what others may think (anyone who has taken a service in a mental hospital will recognize the point). They live more simply in the present moment, their humility and transparency making them naturally disposed towards community festivity. 'The handicapped person,' said one of the participants in our colloquium, also, 'helps us discover our own identity. Our gifts and competence are never adequate and they transform these in order that we may respond to their real needs; we thereby discover who we are.'

It is possible for the disabled to be the victims of other people's need to organize, dominate, or do miracles. God does not organize, dominate, or do miracles for Ann. God lets her be. Perhaps she ministers to God. I know in myself that the disabled exercise an important ministry to the ordinary. Students at St John's may reckon from time to time that the principal is a so-and-so: as well as having institutional power that I can misuse, I can beat them in an argument most of the time if I choose to do so. As I suggested in the Introduction, imagine what a so-and-so I might have been if it were not for the positive shaping effect on me of Ann's disability. I know she slows me down, for good; often we will be processing through the college dining room with half the college behind us, but I have the impression no one minds. She makes me appreciate simple things, like squirrels and clouds and the swaying of the willow tree outside our house. At l'Arche 'the basic mode of existence is by necessity contemplative rather than activist' and that offers an important witness regarding the nature of theology, church, and world.

There is another shaping too. My pain can wash over into my functioning in college in a negative way. One of my best friends once called me 'volatile', unpredictable in how I may react depending on how I am inside. Ann's illness frees both tears and frustration, both love and anger, both resilience and guilty powerlessness ('Why can't I make it OK?'). Giving yourself to the poor or disabled, someone at l'Arche commented, can be the equivalent of going into the solitude of the desert to allow ourselves to be confronted by the demons within.

It is often hard to convince Ann of the positive effect she has on other people or on me. Indeed I myself am not sure exactly what is the nature of that effect, as I do not know who I would be if I were not Ann's husband, shaped by who she is. We and God use her, without scruple (as Paul has God reaffirming, 'I will have mercy on whom I have mercy and will have compassion on whom I have compassion'). We and God gain from her disability. For her there is often no felt gain. It is wholly loss. I trust that God grieves over that as well as using her. Apparently God does not mind such waste; God has some other concern.

Someone during the weekend said, 'The handicapped person helps us discover our own identity. Our gifts and competence are never adequate and they transform these in order that we may respond to their real needs; we thereby discover who we are. In addition they discover what they are by what they call forth in us.' I dearly wish all this to be true, and believe it is true up to the last sentence; it is not clear to me that that last sentence is true. Ann now has less comprehension of who she is than she had ten years ago, and little comprehension of what she calls forth in people (except when I keep telling her). We must no more romanticize the disabled than marginalize them.

Over tea on the Sunday afternoon that weekend I made a point of having a conversation with Frances Young, one of its organizers, whose severely disabled son is the subject of her book *Face to Face*. I wanted to say how much I had appreciated the opportunity for the first time to talk about Ann and me in the presence of people who knew from their own analogous experience what I meant. She gave me an awesomely fierce hug and said something like 'I hope there will be something positive for you in the end'. They were almost the last words that were said to me before we left, and they were going round in my head and my heart for the next thirty-six hours. They somehow brought to the surface a hopelessness which I myself feel about Ann and which I had not quite confessed to myself but had apparently communicated in my 'testimony'(!). Now I feel like John Cleese (in a wonderful moment in the film *Clockwise*, I think), when he says, 'It's not the despair I can't stand, it's the hope'. (Actually, I subsequently discovered that what Frances said to me over tea was that she hoped I had gained something positive out of the weekend; I think Freud commented on how significant our mishearings are . . .)

I refer to hopelessness in this age, of course. The fact that Ann will be raised in Jesus to dance in the New Jerusalem is important to both of us. I once used to say to students that I would not mind if Bultmann was right that this life is all we have, but I no longer say that. Yet I must not give the wrong impression even about this age. One day I cried out to God as I stood in my study, looking out over the courtyard, 'I can't do it,' and God replied, 'You'll just have to.' That sounds hard but in a strange way came as reassurance; it reminds me now of Gerhard von Rad's emphasis on the revelation of the torah to Israel being a gift rather than an imposition. If God lays an expectation on you, it will not be one impossible to fulfil. Since then I have often cried out, 'Will it be all right?' and always known God say, 'Yes'. And it always has been.

On the way to Dover on the Friday an apologetic policeman spot-fined me for speeding on the A2. By contrast, I could drive from the Calais hoverport to Paris in two hours without breaking the speed limit. On the way back to the Channel on the Sunday evening, to the left was the most spectacular golden, red, yellow and orange sunset, to the right darkness and gloom over the Pays de Calais slagheaps, in front a massive cloudbank over the Channel, beneath the cloudbank a sea which felt less rough than the hoverport said it was, and behind it some English rain. Some things depend on perspective, but not everything.

(iv) Born to run?

In his comments on Bruce Springsteen in *Hungry for Heaven*, Steve Turner suggests that a tension between humanity's 'heavenly calling' and 'earthly imprisonment' is the theme of Springsteen's best work. 'In a typical small-town situation he sees two different sorts of people. There are those who resign themselves to mediocrity and those who burn with a passion to transcend their circumstances.'

In my last St John's gig I sang 'Born to Run' to further student bemusement. With wonderful melodrama it relates the way someone whose life feels hopeless urges 'Wendy' to get out of this empty town with him, to let him in to be her friend and guard her 'dreams and visions', to join him in going somewhere where they can walk in the sun, and in the meantime 'live with the sadness. But till then tramps like us, baby we were born to run.'

But 'having articulated a religious question, he doesn't have a religious answer. Springsteen, I believe, realizes that a religious answer is needed and compensates by dressing essentially existential advice in glorious heavenly language' (Turner). In contrast, Christians have the religious answer, but often don't articulate the question.

9

Identity

I have talked about the release we experience when we put down a burden and let our tensed muscles relax, and the way it may be only then that we realize that we were carrying a heavy load. The experience of doing this can also raise questions of identity, for our carrying responsibilities is integral to identity for many of us.

A few years ago Ann and I had our first fortnight's holiday together on our own after our two sons had grown up, and somehow it brought home to me a frightening realization about who I was – namely Ann's husband. At centre I was not a theologian or a teacher or a minister or a scholar or a principal – those were not what defined who I was. Who I was was the husband of this disabled person. That was what shaped my life and my being as nothing else did. Which means, I realized (and this was the frightening bit), that when Ann dies, I shall not know who I am. This does not imply that I have reason to think that she may die soon; she may well outlive me. People with multiple sclerosis have shorter life expectancy than other people, but men have shorter life expectancy than women, so those two considerations rather cancel each other out. The point was that thinking about Ann's eventual death raised this question for me.

I realized that threatening fact anew when she had her seizure. When she was admitted to hospital, a neurologist reassured me that she would fully recover, but as she lay in a bed unable to move, except for the one arm which flapped about with a mind of its own, that was not easy to believe. The nursing staff did not believe it either ('I don't think she will ever feed herself again,' one said). For that matter the neurologist later told me that he was not sure he had believed his own words, but I guess he was going by the book, and he was right. Indeed, some weeks after leaving hospital Ann actually had more mobility than she had before her seizure. Someone told me of a woman in the USA who was cured of multiple sclerosis through being struck by lightning (I have not sought out thunderstorms to see if we can repeat the trick); perhaps Ann's seizure had a little of the same effect.

But in those dark early morning hours when I did not know what was happening, I wondered if she was dying. In those early days in hospital I again found myself thinking the selfish thought that if she died I would not know who I was, because my identity (I felt) was defined by her. Of course in a way this question arises no more in this particular relationship than it does for all of us because of the way our relationships shape us. Who would I be if I did not have this responsibility? If I think of 'me' separately from Ann, what do I mean by the notion of 'me'?

If I answered, 'Who I might be is a good-looking man with a full head of brown hair,' it might make the idea of not having the burden attractive. But it makes me feel insecure. Many years ago, before we knew that Ann might one day be wheelchair-bound, we knew a man whose wife had a chronic illness and was wheelchair-bound. He always looked dishevelled and ill-shaven, but I thought that was just the way he was as a person. Then we lost touch with them, and his wife died, and after a year or two he married again. Shortly after that we met him again, and he was transformed into someone who looked smart and bright and alive. I wonder whether there is some sense in which I am at the former stage. My friends do not recognize the portrait, but I still wonder how things would be different. I know that Ann is a different person from the one she once was, and so am I.

Ann's being in hospital after her seizure meant that I had to come into our main college midweek supper on my own. Instead of walking in with her on my arm, I walked in alone. I felt a stranger in a strange place. Without Ann I did not know who I was, because she shapes who I am. As I have hinted already, any husband or wife does that to a degree, but it feels as if this is true in a distinctive way because who I am is the husband of someone who has this grim illness, and because the handling of that is so central in the shaping of my life. Being without Ann and imagining what it would be like if that were ever a permanent condition made we realize that I was not sure who I really was or whether I really existed. Are we only a series of potentials that become realized, but only in part, in relation to the people we become involved with and the experiences that happen to us? If so I could have been realized in some other way. And the potentials are still there – I could still be realized in other ways. So who is this 'I'?

Oddly, however, living virtually without Ann for those four weeks and living and relating to other people in new ways also strangely reassured me that there is a person here who exists in his own right, a person who one day I might find myself getting to know, but who perhaps for the moment is suppressed. To adapt Brian Keenan's wonderful image, Humpty Dumpty had to stay as he was for the moment; the extra pieces had to remain in store.

I was thinking about all this when one day I heard the Jimmy Cliff song 'Many Rivers to Cross'. It is the original version of one of the classic reggae songs, rawer than UB40's which is perhaps better-known, but less melodramatic than Joe Cocker's. For me that perhaps gives it more quiet power. Out of interest, and perhaps with a view to singing it one day, I settled down to work out all the words. I soon found myself in tears over them because they expressed so much of what I was feeling about life at that time. There are many rivers to cross and 'it's only my will that keeps me alive'. Maybe 'I merely survive because of my pride'. And the loneliness won't leave me alone because the person I once knew is gone, and all sorts of temptations assail me, but I just have to keep looking for a way to cross rivers.

I think there is a link between this and a picture which has developed in my mind. I see myself pushing Ann's wheelchair toward the horizon. I am viewing us from behind, so I see my back and a bit of the wheelchair – I cannot actually see Ann. It is a bare landscape and there is quite a distance to the horizon towards which I push, but the ground is fairly level and the pushing just requires commitment, grit and persistence. A key point is that the distance to the horizon is finite and that I cannot see how far the journey goes beyond the horizon. In theory there may be many horizons to travel (many rivers to cross), but I do not have to visualize or face the fact of that long a journey – just the one horizon. Perhaps that may be the only one, so that the pushing ends just beyond the visible horizon. The other key point is that there are only the two of us, and there is thus only me pushing. A single horizon and a lone push – on my own by my willpower I can just manage one horizon at a time, not quite facing the things that Jimmy Cliff expresses.

The alternative picture which has started to nudge itself upon me has two elements to it. First, my viewpoint changes in the vertical plane – I zoom up, as happens in a film when the camera is elevated on a camera crane. The horizon lengthens vastly, and I can see that the journey, the push, is much, much longer than I can see from ground level. There are indeed many rivers. There is no longer any avoiding the prospect of the push lasting ten or twenty years, not just two or five (and it may become more mountainous, too).

The other element is that the camera descends back to near ground level and I see other people, in ones and twos and threes, coming to join me behind the wheelchair. (I cry as I write this bit.) Some are people I know, some are people I do not yet know, some are people I have known. Some just walk with me. Some take a handle. Some gently push me out of the way and push the wheelchair themselves. Ann is content as long as someone is pushing. (That seems important: it places a question mark over my assumption of indispensability, which is part of my identity.) I walk with them in the little crowd, content, more relaxed, unaccustomed to the luxury of walking without pushing. (I cry some more.) We talk quite a bit and laugh quite a bit. Someone ruffles my hair. The people change – some walk alongside for longer than others. The number of them changes – sometimes there are one or two, sometimes eight or ten. From where I am, because of the other people I can no longer see whether the countryside is bare, nor am I so aware of the distance to the horizon(s) or of how far we travel. I can now commit myself to the ten or twenty years while living in the present more, rather than being tempted to postpone living till some future which may never come.

I once compared notes with another 'single carer' and we discussed the question whether it was too risky to become dependent on there being other people there to help, because you have to be able to cope if the chips are down and you are on your own. I guess the picture summons me to the risk.

One of the results of Ann's seizure was indeed that some people forced their way into my life out of love for me and for her. When I have a bout of 'flu like the one which caught me when she was ill, I like to hide away on my own until I feel better; I do not appreciate people trying to look after me. The kind of people who like being looked after no doubt are the kind who try to look after others in that situation, and such people used to ignore the notices I put on my door saying I was in bed (because they had peered round the back and discovered that I was not) and offered those strange signs of caring, bringing me college food (actually college food is rather good, but I was not up to eating much).

That forcing their way into our lives continued after the crisis was over. It might have been tempting to assume that people were sorry for us and/or were being 'pastoral', and if that had been so, I would still have appreciated it. (In another context a theological college lecturer whose marriage had broken up described to me how someone who taught pastoral theology at his college spent time with him every week for months as he coped with his grief. I remember thinking that this showed that pastoral care was not merely something this teacher taught as theory.) But it became clear that these people who forced their way into our lives were not merely feeling sorry for me or being pastoral but were doing so because they liked me.

I feel self-conscious writing that last phrase, which is significant because I do not very often feel self-conscious about anything. I have noted that embarrassment is one of those capacities that were left out when I was born. I know I have the capacity to be vulnerable in a way that lots of people cannot. I do not mind crying in public (which is as well, because often I cannot avoid it). In teaching and preaching and writing I have come to make a point of verbalizing anxieties and a sense of inadequacy because I know that these feelings are not peculiar to me. Other people feel them, but because they are less insensitive than I am, they may not express them. So I hope this frees them to get their own demons out of their cupboards. I guess it is my own experience of something which I think I see happening with Ann. In her weakness and vulnerability she embodies what most of us feel we are inside. She brings these demons out into the open and thereby exorcises them.

But there is something paradoxical here. When there was discussion of whether I should be made principal, and for that matter on at least one earlier occasion when there had been discussion of whether I should be 'promoted' to some position of further responsibility within college, the difficulty was raised that I can be defensive and aggressive. In meetings or lectures I put people down, without realizing what I am doing. That suggests that I lack inner strength and confidence. Yet being able to be open about weakness implies some inner strength or confidence. What is the relationship between the strength that makes it possible to be open about weakness, and the weakness that makes it necessary to assert strength? Perhaps it is that in the former case I am in control – I choose to let myself cry (more or less). In the latter case other people are seeking to set the agenda and I am not so clearly in control.

Another reason why I may be aggressive in this way is that I tend to take my strong points for granted and only take my weaknesses seriously. (A student once commented that she thought it was only women who did that!) Recognizing this, I have been able to grow a little with regard to it. Now I can admit the weaknesses in my strengths too, and have become more able in a good sense to believe in and live on the basis of the strong points, to be myself and shrug my shoulders more. Where I would once have been hurt by the exposure of some failure in one of the 'strong' areas, now I am better at acknowledging it and regretting it without being chewed up by it.

In the capacity for defensiveness and aggressiveness I have more of a problem with men than with women, and I think women find me easier than men do. There is a fascinating book by Richard Olivier called *Shadow of the Stone Heart* (Pan, 1995) about his 'search for manhood' which began with the death of his father, the actor Laurence Olivier. At one level I saw only contrast between my relationship with my father and his relationship with his, and yet his reflections helped me to see something about my own experience and my own identity. I was past thirty when my father died. It happened when he was sixty-five but it happened quite suddenly, and afterwards I kept saying, 'But I never knew him' – and now it was too late. I thought I meant 'I didn't know what he was like, I didn't know what made him tick', because he was a private or shy person. But I was talking about Olivier's book with a friend, and she asked (because of a question she had been thinking about), 'Do you think we ever really know anyone else, or are known by them?' In an ultimate sense that may be true, but we do grow in knowledge. It has been a paradoxical thing which I have come to realize with regard to one or two people, that the more I have got to know them, the less I know them in the sense of being able to sum them up simply, in a list of epithets, as I might have done when I did not know them. It is the same with God.

But the question about whether we ever really know someone made me realize that I did not (just) mean that I did not have much insight into my father, but that we had never really been friends. I wondered whether I had failed to make the same transfer from mother to father that Olivier failed to make (without my being stony-hearted as he sees himself to have been – at least I am not that now). And I wondered whether that was why it seemed to be men who were usually a threat to me rather than women. I also wondered whether my first vicar, whose comment on the Psalms I mentioned in Chapter 1, was in Olivier's terms my mentor, the person who is not your father but who helps you on your way to manhood. He had himself once said that when your father died you became a man; and I recalled this observation, when my father indeed died, with some puzzlement because I did not feel anything of that. But soon afterwards, this vicar of mine himself became ill, and I visited him in hospital, and soon afterwards he died; and I remember feeling that then I became a man. (And I wondered about my sons and their relationship to me as their father.)

Somewhere here there are links with things that go back to childhood, as is the case with many of our adult oddities. I came from an ordinary 'upper working class' background in Birmingham. No one in my family had ever been to grammar school, let alone to the most prestigious school in the city. When I went there, I was on my own, and I certainly felt on my own. My family could not help me with this experience, I thought, because they had not been there. I had to be able to cope, to be self-sufficient, and to do that without reference to my father or mother because they had not been this way. My father and I could not become friends.

At this school it was academic achievement that counted. When I gained a place at Oxford, there was no danger of pride, because there were a dozen or twenty people who got scholarships to Oxbridge from our school. I failed to do that, so I hardly counted. Even now, getting an article or a book published is important but it does not seem so much of an achievement; it is simply what I do.

But discovering that someone likes spending time with me gives me a quite different buzz. Over a period of a year or two I began to get used to the idea that some people enjoyed my company. I remember a particular conversation with a person who felt the same way as I did and was hesitant (for instance) about just calling in to see someone on the assumption that one would be welcome. I knew that I would be welcomed in the sense that people would want to do that pastoral, Christian thing because I was a person in need. But I was not sure that I would be welcome in the more general sense – welcome just because of who I was. We agreed that we would always welcome each other in the second of those senses!

What is it that makes me, or anyone else, or God, attractive to me or to anyone else or to God? Again there are paradoxes here. If we are describing a friend to someone, we probably refer to some attributes. By implication, I enjoy that person's company because he is sensitive or fun or because he likes rock and roll or is an interesting theologian. Yet it is not actually a specifiable list of attributes (or only one that goes on until infinity) that draws us into friendship with people. It is more something like an intuitive sense that there is someone attractive here. Perhaps everyone is likeable in this sense – the question is whether that likeableness is on the surface or is recognized, or whether it is hidden.

There is then an important dialectical relationship between knowing and loving. Having begun to know, I begin to love. Beginning thus to love, I get to know more because the other person is more willing to be known. Getting to know more, I love more because I understand more. Loving more, I get to know more. And that goes on for ever. And this is true of relations among human beings, between us and God, and between me and me.

If the knowing is not merely having a list of attributes, what is it? To judge from the way the Bible works, as well as to conform to a trendy current insight, it involves narrative. The knowing comes about through listening to stories. When we want to characterize each other, we will often do so by telling a story that sums the person up. (My story about the cheesecake and the chocolate bar in chapter 1 was designed to sum up something about what Ann does to people, but it also sums up the person of our host that day.)

In the Bible, God is known as one who has certain attributes. The classic list comes first in Exodus 34 and often recurs: it is that Yahweh is compassionate and gracious, long-tempered and abounding in love and faithfulness, maintaining love and forgiving shortcomings, though in the end not soft. But that characterization of God comes in the midst of a gargantuan narrative that extends from Genesis to Kings, and then in the midst of further narratives in Chronicles, Ezra-Nehemiah, Esther, Ruth, Jonah, and elsewhere. Those narratives do all sorts of things, but one thing they do is establish who God is. Stories do that. They give life to adjectives and nouns.

The list in Exodus 34 shows that there is something to be said for adjectives and nouns. There is a significant overall picture painted by the stress on God's friendly side, for instance, but a significant solemn addition in the refusal to omit the tough side. And I have found that the same is true about human characterization.

After a number of sessions with the counsellor to whom I referred in Chapter 6, eventually he and I began to wonder whether we had done the main business, and whether we were to go anywhere else from here or simply call it a day. About that time it happened that we had a time of prayer for healing in a college chapel service, and I felt compelled to go out for prayer. The way the system worked was that it was usual to say just a sentence or two about what you wanted prayer for to the couple who were praying for you, and I said that I actually felt odd about doing this because I was more in a mood for thanksgiving for what God had done both for Ann and for me than feeling the need for prayer.

The person who prayed with me said that she felt that I had a barrier like a shield around me preventing access. Precisely because of what I have said about vulnerability, I was surprised. I thought that whatever faults I might have, shutting people out was not one of them. She wondered whether what it might mean (that is, as often happens, the picture was what she was given, but the interpretation was her guess) was that the shield was there not to keep other people out but to keep me out. What God was inviting me to do was to discover who I was, to let myself into myself. (I wonder now whether the ease of letting other people see what made me tick – no doubt selectively, as I suggested in Chapter 1 – was a cover for avoiding doing that myself.) I was immediately clear what the counselling agenda needed to be. As I have said, over recent years I have grown or changed, not least through coping with Ann. My identity is thus tied up with her. What I am is her husband. I said that to a friend once, and was rebuked with the reminder that I was someone in myself. God was now bidding me discover who that was.

A day or two later, I had to compose a paragraph about myself for some purpose. Such paragraphs usually go 'The Revd Dr John Goldingay is Principal of St John's College, Nottingham. He has written a number of books on the Old Testament. He is married to Ann, who has multiple sclerosis.' As I have hinted, I have been tempted to think that in real terms all it need say is the last sentence. That is who I am. I decided to try to say who I was irrespective of work and in myself, and began 'John Goldingay is an enthusiast about rock, blues, and jazz'.

I told all this to the counsellor. When I got to the last bit he shot bolt upright in his chair. That was significant in itself. I noted earlier that he is the kind of counsellor who normally sits impassive and unreactive; it is extremely frustrating and extremely effective. This time he shot up and said, 'Yes! You're an enthusiast.' Now in my mind the stress had been on what I was enthusiastic about, but he showed me another, more important implication of what I had written. There was something about my personality there in the word 'enthusiast'. And I could immediately recognize it, though I had not seen it as clearly before.

This is both an example of the usefulness of adjectives and nouns and also somehow an example of loving and thus knowing. Although the counsellor would sit there impassive and unreactive because that helped the counselling process, I knew that this did not signify coldness. I think I knew that he loved me. His uncharacteristic outburst was an expression of love, the more powerful because of its rarity, and of love which had issued in insight for him and thus in insight for me. I remember feeling that I had had set in front of me the empty outline of the shape of a person, like a child's drawing, and that I now had the first word, the first attribute, to put inside it.

For a while I had a hard time finding other words to put into the person-shaped blank. I can think of two reasons for that. One is that some, like 'vulnerability', are related to Ann, and I wanted to find things that were not contingent on that relationship. The other is that I did not quite dare to believe the words, even when they came from other people. I guess this is one reason why I am not going to list them all here, but just the next five: imaginative, colourful, physical, unassuming, dangerous. I especially like the last, which, as I have mentioned, was our bass-player's description of me as lead-singer, but I will comment on just the first of those. I think I may be able now to believe more deeply that I am imaginative as well as analytical. I have had people say that and I can sense it in myself, but at first I did not really dare believe it. After all, if I did believe that I had positive qualities, the descriptions might then turn out to be wrong, and my inner suspicion that there is little positive to say about me would be powerfully reinforced. So the risk was too great.

Because of something one of our students happened to say over lunch, I told him about the visit to the counsellor and about discovering that I was an enthusiast. The college is named after St John the Evangelist, and the student later told me he had been thinking about 'St John the Enthusiast', as an equivalent to St John the Evangelist. That made me remember that 'enthusiast' comes from a Greek word which would mean 'filled with God' or 'inspired', and that my enthusiasm could be something from God and through which God worked. The same is true of being imaginative and creative, because God is the very source of imagination and creativity. So discovering things about identity could be not merely something which made a neurotic person feel a bit better, but something which related to my living for God.

One example: I used to get angry with Ann when I felt she slighted me – when she seemed to talk to me as if I was incredibly stupid for misunderstanding her. 'Where are we?' she asked as we left a motorway restaurant. 'Near Weston-super-Mare,' I replied. 'I mean where is the car,' she retorted. I then tore strips off her for talking to me as if I was dirt and I told her never to do it again, and she got angry and cried. Before we went to bed we made up, but I knew it was an example of something that happens from time to time. Her frustration with her lot finds transferred expression in hostility to me, and for some reason I find it difficult to cope with that particular expression of it. Eventually I realized it was because it hooks memories from childhood (not that my mother ever intended to be scathing, any more than Ann does). Now I have realized that this is what happens, I am less vulnerable to it. So discovering things about identity could even be something which relates to my living with other people.

10

Joy

'You will have joy and gladness, and many will rejoice at his birth,' the angel said to Zechariah (Luke 1:14). And when his wife saw Mary, the baby in her womb 'leaped for joy' (1:44). When John was born, her neighbours and relatives 'shared her joy' (1:57). And when the angels appeared to the shepherds, they brought them news of 'great joy' for everyone (2:10).

So what is joy? First, let us not be rude about noisiness. The kind of rejoicing that the Bible talks most of is a noisy affair. It is a matter of celebration, loud music, shouting, dancing. When there is joy about, it can be heard a long way away. Joy is associated with harvest and winning battles, with feasting and drinking. Modern books on spirituality tend to imply that spirituality is an 'introvert' business (in the Myers-Briggs sense). They talk about going to the depths and about the journey inward, and so on. Most of the time the Bible's spirituality of joy is an 'extrovert' spirituality. So it is a spirituality for the majority, an asset in mission and ministry, an invitation to your shadow side.

But many Christians are introverts, and maybe need to start somewhere else. In odd corners of the Bible introverts can find a joy for them. Here is Psalm 4:7: 'You have filled my heart with greater joy than when their grain and new wine abound.' Jeremiah, that great introvert, wrote: 'Your words . . . were my joy and my heart's delight' (15:16). I suppose it is a sign of the dominance of introvert spirituality that we think of joy as a matter of the heart. It is closely related to peace, I think. Peace is an inner acceptance of things, but it is more passive than joy.

Joy is an inner liftedness of spirit that means we do more than just cope inside when things are tough; we are happy inside even if things are hard outside. Inside us and in private our hands are raised in worship. How can that be?

One summer someone said to me, 'You're not bad at producing the fruit of the Spirit really, except joy, you're not very good at joy.' It made me think, of course. I knew that I was often morose, for personality and circumstantial reasons, and not very good at hiding my feelings, and I do not think I had quite seen moroseness and joy as something to bring to God. So I did. I asked God for a spirit of joy. And God gave me that, for much of the latter part of that summer. Humanly speaking, that was possible because there had been some holiday and I had shed responsibility. Then, when I had to take on responsibilities again, joy went. So I asked God to give it back, not expecting that to work, and God did. And it went again under pressure, but I knew that was in part because of neglect, and I thought I had to say goodbye and accept that this was all my fault. But I asked for it back once more, not expecting that to work, and again God gave it back to me.

In the end that fitted with something I learned through a book about Galatians, which saw the key to Galatians as the question whether people were trying to continue by means of the flesh, when they began by means of the Spirit. If joy is a gift, a fruit of the Spirit's presence, there is no reason why God should not give it at any moment. It is not dependent on my persistence or failure, but on God's giving. Not that I did nothing: I did sing through a lot of praise songs on my own on two or three occasions. But that would have got nowhere without God's giving. And perhaps that might be true for anyone, with joy or with whatever gift or fruit we would like. If we are serious about these things being God's gifts and not dependent on us, we might even ask God to give them to us.

There is a wonderful Glasgow band called 'The Blue Nile'. They are perfectionists and they release an album only once every six years. 1996's was called *Peace at Last*. The title track asks the question, 'Now that I've found peace at last, tell me Jesus, will it last? Now that I've found peace of mind, tell me Jesus, is it mine?'

I've begun to believe that the answer might be 'Yes'. As Habakkuk puts it, 'Though the fig tree does not bud and there are no grapes on the vines, though the olive crop fails and the fields produce no food, though there are no sheep in the pen and no cattle in the stalls, yet I will rejoice in Yahweh, I will be joyful in God my saviour' – if he gives me the gift.

On one of the occasions when I was in between joys, I was out running and feeling that nevertheless things were quite good with the world really and in that sense I was quite happy. But I told myself that this did not count as joy in the Lord. It was just natural light-heartedness, of which I have quite a lot interwoven with a capacity for being morose. Then in the first week of term, we had a meditation in chapel about the story of the woman anointing Jesus' feet, which provoked a Pharisee to query whether she had any business to be making an offering to Jesus.

We were asked who were the people who found fault with our offerings; and I knew that the only person who found fault with my offering was me. I did not think I had anything worth offering. I knew that this was daft and that although I did not believe in my gift to Jesus, he believed in it and rejoiced in it. I did not know why I did not believe I had anything to offer Jesus that he would value, and neither at that moment did I know what my offering might be. Only a bit later did I realize that my natural light-heartedness might be part of it. It did not constitute joy, but if I gave it to God, it was transformed into joy, it became a rejoicing in the Lord of the kind that Philippians 4 speaks of, and it was an offering Jesus was happy to receive and consecrate. In general, I believe that spiritual gifts and fruits are natural capacities released and brought out and brought to fulfilment and utilized to glorify Christ by the Spirit, and this was just one example.

Then there was an occasion when I was running round the field feeling joyful at 7.45 a.m. It was the day I was due to take Ann to the rehabilitation centre for a stay – it was a scheduled stay, not because there was a problem, though one did manage to emerge. Yet as I was putting her into the car I found myself crying, and I knew it was because that sort of moment brings home to me the reality of her illness. Whereas we try to live a 'normal' life, a moment like that reminds me of the sadness of how things actually are. That did not surprise me. What did surprise me was that juxtaposition of joy and tears. It should not have surprised me, because that is how our life is, and how most human life is; I suspect. Quite often it is joy alternating with sadness. Weeping may remain for the night, but rejoicing comes in the morning (Psalm 30:5).

Some of us feel uncomfortable with the one, some with the other, some with either. Even if our own lives seem to be one or the other, in the lives of people near us there is bound to be the one we have not got. And maybe we then feel bad about the one we have got, whether it is sadness or joy, or find it hard to handle the fact that the other person has the opposite. God calls us to rejoice with those who rejoice and weep with those who weep, which may among other things mean that we are able to hold both together in ourselves, or at least to let them alternate, not be unrealistically stuck in one or the other.

When I realized that I did not believe that anything I could give Jesus was worthwhile, that he could be enthusiastic about anything I brought, I knew that there was something more afoot than merely not being able to recognize the value of a particular gift. Behind that was a more general uncertainty about me and God. I find it easy to identify with the woman who only wanted to touch the edge of Jesus' coat to access the healing power, and then hide so as not to cause too much trouble. God did once convince me of love and welcome for me, but I had evidently lost sight of that for a time. One morning when I was not especially thinking about this but was just having a quiet time, I was suddenly overwhelmed by joy as God pointed to something in me and in effect said, 'Do not you see how I rejoice at that, at the way you give yourself to me in that,' looking at me in love because I was doing my best in my feebleness, and I found myself in tears and in joy at the same time.

And joy is often like that, is it not? It involves tears because it brings out into the open your deepest fears, the anxieties you most hide from, which it can do because it is confronting them and demonstrating that they are unfounded, and therefore that you can laugh and weep at the same time. You rejoice when things are tough, and you weep when things are great. The two are interwoven. When people returning from Babylon began to restore the temple, 'No one could distinguish the sound of the shouts of joy from the sound of weeping' (Ezra 3:13) because they felt both sadness and joy. That was true in the community. It is often true for the individual. They do not just alternate. They are there at the same time.

So many things we achieve are achieved only through struggle and conflict, not in easy ways. They always seem to involve crosses. I have so longed to find somewhere in life some corner where joy is unmingled with pain. But I have never found it. Wherever I find joy, my own or other people's, and I do, it always seems to be mingled with pain. I still hanker after there being a corner of reality somewhere where there is joy that is unrelated to pain, some other universe where that is true, some charismatic experience that is simply joy. I long to escape into it. But I cannot locate it. And I find that the people I most respect are people who know the link between joy and pain. And I know that God has given me moments of great joy and praise, but they have always been related to pain and hurt and loss, my own or other people's. And I have found that if we will own pain and weep over it together, we also find that Christ is overflowing comfort. The bad news is that there may be no corner of reality where joy is not related to pain. The good news is that there is no corner of reality where pain cannot be transformed into overflowing joy.

There was another penny that dropped for me at about the same time. It was to do with the sequence in Galatians 5. 'The fruit of the Spirit is love, joy, peace . . .' It suggests that joy flows from love. You might have thought that it flowed from being loved, and of course that is true. Galatians opens up the other possibility, that joy flows from loving, from giving love.

God does not ask us to love everyone. There is not enough of us. God does ask us to love a few people. You can give lots of yourself to one or two or three people. You can pour out yourself for them, like that woman with her bottle of perfume. The word 'joy' does not come in that story, but the story does indicate that because she poured herself out in love, she found forgiveness and salvation and peace, which are not unrelated to joy. Of course she did not earn her forgiveness or her salvation that way. She was already responding to the way Jesus had reached out to people and to what she knew was for her too. But it all became actual for her, the forgiveness and the salvation and the peace and the joy, because she gave the most precious thing she had in love. And not because that was her motivation, because then it would not have worked. She did it because she loved.

In John 15 Jesus talks about love and joy, and in five verses he uses the word 'love' eight times. In the middle of them he says, 'I have told you this so that my joy may be in you and that your joy may be complete.' His joy came from his loving, and so would theirs.

One Monday morning when Ann was going down with a bug, though I did not know that this was what was happening (but I thought that something was happening), I woke up and found myself saying to God, 'I do not trust you with Ann.' Then before I could get struck by lightning I said, 'Well, in some ultimate sense I do trust you. I know it will be all right at the End. The problem is what you might let happen in the meantime.' I have to let the trust which can hold for the End hold for the meantime. In other words, the fact that the Lord is at hand means that I can have a kind of anticipatory joy in the present when it is not the End.

In Philippians 4 it is not clear what Paul meant when he linked 'Rejoice in the Lord always' with 'the Lord in near'. It is not clear what he sees as the link between the successive clauses. The Church of England reads this passage in Advent, which invites us to assume, plausibly, that Christ's second coming is a reason for joy in the 'now'.

I mentioned in Chapter 8 how I used to say that I would not mind if Bultmann was right and the Second Coming was a myth, but now I do mind. Here is another reason, that it matters that Jesus is going to finish the job he has begun, a job of putting down evil and restoring rightness. Both may have been begun. Neither is finished. The Bible assumes that both will be reason for great joy when they are achieved, and that means that we have reason for anticipatory joy now. I can trust God with Ann because I know God will finish.

Incidentally I knew that God was saying back to me, 'If you were me, would you trust you with Ann?' and that the answer was 'No'. But God is committed to the risk business, knowing an inner commitment on the part of Father, Son and Holy Spirit to complete what is begun and fulfil the plan. The Second Coming is important to God, too. God's purpose is on the line. So we can rejoice, because the Lord is at hand.

11

Life

(i) Death

I have mentioned the occasion when late one night on holiday in the Alps after a lovely day out and a lovely meal, two friends and I were discussing death. I suppose that originally we must have been discussing something else, though I cannot remember what, but we somehow came to be discussing death, and two of us agreed that it was really quite an attractive prospect. It would be a relief. The third thought this was just bizarre.

For me, it had something to do with being tired. The wonderful thing about this holiday was that it became a fortnight in which responsibilities were shed, burdens shared and furrows fell away from brows, and by the end I may not have felt the same about the attractiveness of death; I cannot remember. I do remember that it was hard to pick up the burdens and responsibilities again after the holiday.

Death is entirely natural. There is a natural sequence that takes us from conception and birth through growth to maturity through senescence to death and nothingness. It is not frightening or sad or incomplete. It is like a novel or a play with a beginning, a middle and an end.

So what happens when we die? We do not cease to exist: you can see the person there, lying on a bed or somewhere. To be more dramatic, imagine it is a couple of teenagers who were full of life a moment ago but lost control of their car on a bend and now they are still there, they still exist, but they are lifeless. They cannot move. They cannot do anything. As the Bible sees it, what happens to us inside is the same as what happens to us outside. Our personality still exists as our body still exists, but our personality becomes lifeless, energy-less, as our body does.

If we were lucky (in the old days, at least), people would open the family tomb and we would be 'laid to rest' with our family, a spouse or parents or grandparents. That was the plan for Princess Diana, though in the event they changed their mind because they thought this tomb at the church would be too accessible to 'pilgrims'. If we are buried in a family tomb, it is not lonely there, but it is dark and lifeless. We are only on the edge of the church now: we cannot join in its worship as we once did. The other week I had to preach in a parish church in the middle of a field (not a house in sight: apparently it had been built next to the manor house, but that had long since fallen down; I suppose it is something that the church has long outlasted it). I had to sit in a seat at the south-eastern corner, next to the tomb of Lady Newdigate, Countess of Derby, which had a sculpture of her recumbent form lying on the top. Two cherubic figures are praying in a space underneath her feet. Because she was a Lady she was buried within reach of the Communion Table, but even she could not reach out and receive the bread and wine along with the ordinary people who could do so because the one thing they had over her was that they were alive. She was present for the worship, but she could not join in. This is one of death's great deprivations, as the Bible sees it. There is no joy and laughter in the grave. We join those other lifeless personalities, and gradually we decompose and virtually cease to exist. (Of course modern death and cremation obscure much of that.)

Yet I love the poignant exposition of what death means in Ecclesiastes 9. The trouble is it brings out the downside to death, the way it makes you re-evaluate the significance of life. Death is the great denial, the great nothingness.

Death is the place where there is no hope (verse 1). In life you can keep hoping against hope, keep kidding yourself that there might be a change, keep praying. Where there is life, there is hope. Death is the great realism. There is not going to be healing. There is not going to be reconciliation. There is not going to be conversion. There is no hope. So even a living dog is better off than a dead lion.

Death is the place where there is no knowledge (verse 5). The living know that they will die; I am mortal, therefore I am. The dead know nothing.

And the dead are not known. Death is the place where people are forgotten (verse 5). Yes, there are exceptions. Plato and Aristotle are remembered, Amos and Jeremiah, Caesar and Brutus. But not the ordinary people who wrote out Plato and Aristotle's works and therefore made them available to us, not Amos' wife and Jeremiah's mother, not the people who cooked lunch for Caesar and Brutus, not the people like you and me. They say that one of the reasons why people long to have children, or at least why they regret not having them, is that children mean your name lives on, you live on. I discovered that a John Goldingay married an Ann Goldingay in Birmingham, where I come from, in 1842, exactly a hundred years before I myself was born, and now I have written about them they are not forgotten, but countless thousands of named and unnamed are forgotten.

Death is the place where people have no feelings (verse 6): 'their love, their hate and their jealousy have long since vanished'. Think of the massive, dynamic strength and significance of our loves, our hatreds, and our jealousies, our wants, our passions, our fury. They make us human. In death there will be none of them.

Death is the place where people can do nothing (verse 6). Here one way or another we gain our significance from being able to take part in things, to contribute to discussions and arguments and decision-making. There: none of it. 'In Sheol, where you are going, there is neither working nor planning nor knowledge nor wisdom' (verse 10).

And death is unpredictable (verse 12). 'No one knows when their hour will come: as fish are caught in a cruel net, or birds are taken in a snare, so people are trapped by evil times that fall unexpectedly upon them.'

People sometimes talk as if this is merely 'the Old Testament understanding of death', by which they mean 'the Old Testament's (pardonable) misunderstanding', now corrected by 'the (true) New Testament understanding'. But this Old Testament understanding is right. One look in the tomb establishes it. The Christian instinctively says 'but that's just the body'; the soul, the real person, is safe with God. And that is half-true, but it is not enough. The body is as much the real person as the soul, and if those things are true about the body, then they are true about the person. When resurrection comes, they will not be true, but for the time being, they are.

But I could relish all that. No more hoping (and therefore no more disappointment). No more knowing (and therefore no more knowing the tough things). No more memory (so I can forget). No more feelings (and therefore no more worry about whether I am loved). No more doing (and therefore no more responsibility). Like endless Sunday.

But Ecclesiastes sees the negative side. All this is true of everyone indiscriminately. 'All share a common destiny – the righteous and the wicked, the good and the bad, the clean and the unclean, those who offer sacrifices and those who do not.' So what was the point of being righteous, good, clean, worshipful?

There was a great deal of point, actually. They were worthwhile in their own right. Death does not stop them being so. But it does underline a problem. What if that sequence of birth-growth-maturity-senescence-death does not work out in that neat way? I have referred more than once to a time when I could say that I would not be bothered if the great revisionist theologian Rudolf Bultmann was right and the idea of our being raised from the dead to new life in heaven were a myth. This would be OK. I would have enjoyed my life, it would have had its own plot, its own beginning, middle, and end, and I would be happy enough to bow out when the curtain dropped. And for myself that is still to some extent true. Only to some extent, admittedly. I am more aware now of the force of Jesus' argument in Mark 12:18–27 where he grounds the necessity of resurrection in the fact that God is the God of the living, not of the dead. One of the implications of this is that when God enters into a relationship with people such as Abraham, Isaac, or Jacob, or you or me, that is not likely to turn out to be a merely temporary affair. God does not give up on relationships like that. For Ann and me, each time we have said goodbye to someone who mattered to us as we have been preparing to leave Britain, it has been like another little death. We are who we are because of our friendships with these people, so a bit of us dies when these friendships die in their present form. God is not going to die or let us die like that.

But Ecclesiastes reminds me of another reason why I became less easy-going about Bultmann's view. It is one of the reasons for the development of belief in resurrection within Judaism. It is that otherwise things are so unfair. Dan Cohn-Sherbock has argued in his book *Holocaust Theology* (Marshall, 1989) that belief in a resurrection is essential if Jews are to make sense of the fact of the holocaust, and in so arguing he is repeating the logic that drove many Jewish people to this belief two millennia ago, beginning with the visions in Daniel. In my case, believing that resurrection is important links with Ann in particular. It is important to me that, though confined to a wheelchair now, she will dance in heaven. I respect Ecclesiastes for living a tough faith without that conviction; Jews in his day had no empirical evidence for it, and would not have any such evidence until Jesus rose from the dead. I am glad I live the other side of that resurrection, even though believing in Ann's and mine is still a matter of faith.

There is another aspect to the way we experience death. In one sense, in theory, there is a clear distinction between life and death.

I have watched only one person die: Ann's mother. It was itself both strange and providential. As Ann's mother grew older and passed into her eighties, we wondered how the end might eventually come, and wondered how we might cope with increasing frailness as she lived two hours' drive away and Ann was herself disabled. She came to stay with us one Christmas as usual and between Christmas and New Year we went for the first time to see the film *When Harry Met Sally*. Half-way through, to my annoyance, she felt sick and we had to leave the cinema and go home. Eventually it became clear that she had had a heart attack. At first she seemed to improve, but on New Year's Day in the afternoon the hospital rang to suggest that we come in. I knew what that was code for. By the time we reached her bedside she was unconscious and we sat there for some time – I cannot now remember how long. She was breathing quite loudly, almost snoring. Then I remember a moment when she simply stopped. And I remember thinking, 'That's it'. That was life; this is death.

Yet in another sense life and death overlap and interweave. We talk about feeling deathly. We get 'flu and lie in bed not moving or speaking or eating for a day or two and not wishing to talk to anyone thank-you very much (at least that is what I do) and it is like a little death. We are for a while overwhelmed by fears or depressions or responsibilities or guilts or hatreds and it is like having the soil fall onto the coffin as you lie there in it in the newly dug grave. Or you say all those goodbyes (as I said in Chapter 7) and you feel you are becoming a smaller person each time you say one.

It is as if death has got hold of us while we are still alive. And this is how the Bible sees it. Many of the psalms speak of being in Sheol, that corporate grave which is the non-material equivalent to the material tomb, or speak of having been rescued from Sheol when people were delivered from illness or depression or danger. They speak of being overwhelmed by floods, which are the waters of death. Life and death interweave all right. It reminds me of the lines in T. S. Eliot's poem 'Journey of the Magi' in which Eliot has one of the Wise Men wondering about the link between birth and death and realizing that being involved with Christ's birth had taken them through a kind of death, for things which previously suggested life had now died on them. 'I should be glad of another death', he comments. Is life attractive, or is death attractive?

(ii) Life

But what difference does it make that Jesus came back from death to begin a transformed life? Here are three or four things that happened when we visited California in connection with the possibility of moving there.

Just beforehand, in the furthest southwestern tip of California, and thus of the whole United States, thirty-nine people committed suicide in San Diego in the conviction that the Hale-Bopp comet which was then circling the earth was a harbinger of God's coming to take them to be with him. One reaction to that is to feel astonishment that people should reckon anything so certain that it is worth dying for. Yet in that respect it recalls people in the early Christian church seeking martyrdom. From a Christian angle what is odd is not the fact of the certainty but the lack of a basis for it. The fact of the certainty might make us ask how convinced we ourselves are about matters of life and death. A person who had left the cult told the newspapers, 'We were seekers of what was going on, why were we here, what's the purpose of life.' These people were not crazy Californians, except by adoption. They were people from Ohio and Connecticut who had gone to California from elsewhere on a spiritual pilgrimage, as the ancestors of the California-born had once done, in what the newspaper called 'the great American temptation'. It was a continuation of what brought people to 'the New World' in the first place. But the east coast turned out not to be enough, and the trail led ever westward until it reached the point where there was nowhere else to go until you got to Australasia, and so they looked for life another way and found death.

At about the same time Southern California gave Oscars to the film *The English Patient*. It is the story of a man who has been horrifically injured in an aircraft accident in north Africa in the Second World War. He lies encased in bandages, unable to move. In due course an enemy catches up with him but declines to kill him because that would actually be an act of mercy. He is waiting to die. But in another sense, he says, 'I died ages ago.' He is referring not merely to the near-death of his accident but to an event which preceded that, when he lost the only woman he had loved. He had had to leave her, injured, in a cave in a desert mountain, in order to go to get help, and had been unable to convince people that they should listen to him. But he had promised to return. In what I found to be a rather cold film, though a brilliant one, the point when I became emotionally engaged was when he eventually did return, and gathered his love's body and carried it round the mountain to where he had landed his plane, crying a scream that we see on his lips but do not hear, so that it all the more fills the cinema with its silence. That was when he died, ages ago. (I should add that I discovered this to be a male perspective on the film; not surprisingly, a woman with whom I discussed it found the emotionally-engaging moment was the one when the woman is left to die alone in the cave, as she tries to draw a final picture and her light becomes used up and darkness and cold descend.)

While we were in California we were shown round some houses by a 'realtor' or estate agent. Now, as a clergyman I have never bought a house before, and thus had little experience of estate agents. My impression of them was that they were people who would tell any lies in order to make a sale. Our realtor subverted that slanderous impression. She loved people and she loved property, and she seemed to gain her fulfilment from putting the right property and the right people in touch with each other so that they could then live happily ever after. I do not know whether she saw this as a vocation, but it provided me with a brilliant Christian understanding of this particular secular calling. No doubt this is also a more effective way to make money in the long run, and in a litigious society like the USA perhaps also a safer one.

The week we met her was the week after Easter and she happened to express her anger at the sermon she had heard on Easter Day, a sermon that was geared to communicate to children and the television generation. It had taken up some C. S. Lewis story which perhaps expressed the gospel (indeed, as it was Lewis, no doubt it expressed the gospel), but for her it failed to focus clearly enough on the fact that Jesus was alive.

I was struck by the fierceness of her feelings on this matter, and a bit puzzled by it. Next day while we were out looking at some more properties (though we had already found the right one!) I discovered the background. Eight years previously her eighteen-year-old son had gone off for a drive in the mountains that tower above Pasadena, a little like the Alps or Upper Galilee, had failed to take a bend, and had plunged to the bottom of a ravine. This had happened at about the time when faith in

Christ was becoming a reality to her. Her son's death did not lead her to Christ, nor did it drive her away from Christ, but it did somehow come to constitute one of the key factors in determining what Christ meant for her. She did not quite articulate what this was, but I think it was something to do with things having meaning and life being liveable-with. It was the fact that Christ rose to new life that somehow made it possible to live with the fact of her son's falling to the end of his life. It gave her hope. And that was why she was so concentratedly angry that her Easter sermon had not focused explicitly enough on the fact that Jesus was alive. Because that was what made life possible for her.

She makes me think again of the ending of Job's story, when Job gets re-established with his new life and his new family. I find that students do not like the story's ending; it is too neat and unrealistic, they feel, and they prefer the tough realism of the protesting Job. I admit that the ending does make me feel some further sympathy for Mrs Job; I wonder how she now felt, having by the end borne fourteen sons and six daughters.

But theologically and pastorally the story's coming to an end of that kind promises us that stories do have endings, that our story will have an ending. They do not finish with families decimated, lovers dead and lives broken and empty. The story of Job is realistic for theological reasons that are based in the nature of God but are given grounds by the resurrection of Jesus. Easter means that our stories will have an ending.

There was another fact about Easter that came home to me that week. It is a solemn fact about ministry that it can often seem a deathly business. 'We are hard-pressed ... perplexed ... persecuted ... struck down' in the course of our ministry, says Paul. 'We always carry around in our body the death of Jesus' (2 Corinthians 4:8–10). Yes, death is not something which waits till we die. Easter means we die with Christ, but it also means we live with Christ. I heard a sermon that drew attention to the fact that when Mary thought Jesus was the gardener, she was not wrong. He was not only the first-fruits of the dead, but the gardener producing fruit.

(iii)

I was once told of someone who was said to have 'slipped quietly into heaven'. I'm going like a bat out of hell – to adopt a phrase from Jim Steinman and Meat Loaf. More recently Patti Smith's album *Gone Again* commemorated her husband Fred 'Sonic' Smith on his death. Patti was the 'punk high priestess' whose band followed on the work of Andy Warhol and Velvet Underground.

Now her music is one means of coming to terms with the grief of loss. A profile in the *Guardian* reported her statement that her Jehovah's Witness mother's teaching her to pray was 'the greatest gift she could ever have given me. It was the idea that however bored you may be, you can still go to bed early and you can pray.' Now 'pitched between bearing witness to a living God and proclaiming her violent apostasy, Smith's records and perform-ances can be seen as a struggle with the faith she'd learned as a child – an acting out of the "expansive territory" between her Christian mother and her doubting father'. Her first album began with the line 'Jesus died for somebody's sins, but not mine'.

12

Love

(i)

'You are to love your neighbour as yourself' (Leviticus 19:18). It is a rather ambiguous exhortation. In recent decades it has been understood to mean 'You are to love your neighbour as you love yourself' and it has become a proof-text for the notion of 'loving oneself' as a key to personal health. It is the only such proof-text as far as I know. I cannot think of other scriptures that explicitly encourage us to love ourselves or accept ourselves as we are, though I can think of a few that seem to suggest the opposite.

Now it might be hypothesized that the cultures of the Bible were healthier than ours, that the notion (or rather the reality) of accepting oneself could be taken for granted, and that being prepared to say no to yourself was therefore the point that had to be stressed. But I am generally wary of arguments that suggest that people in the Bible were different from us in the way they worked. In other connections it is important for us to assume that they worked in the same way as we do, and that assumption proves fruitful. It seems at least as likely that our preoccupation with ourselves needs to be confronted rather than accepted. The Bible's emphasis on giving your life away and getting it back as a result provides a different way into the issues involved in the notion of 'loving oneself'. Perhaps we will find more acceptance of ourselves and love for ourselves through giving ourselves away to others than we will find in actually focusing on loving ourselves so that we can work towards loving other people. That way we short-circuit the process. It is in any case uncertain whether 'You are to love your neighbour as yourself' means what has been suggested. It is more likely to mean 'you are to love your neighbour as a person like yourself' (so the New English Bible).

So what is love? The companion exhortation about loving God may give us clues. We are to love God with all our heart, soul, and strength (Deuteronomy 6:5), with all our heart, soul, and mind (Matthew 22:37), with all our heart, soul, mind, and strength (Mark 12:30). The variation reflects differences in the connotations of some of these words in different languages. We have noted in Chapter 5 that in Hebrew the 'heart' denotes what we would call the workings of the mind rather than the emotions, for which you would more likely refer to lower parts of your anatomy (we too speak of a fluttering in the tummy). What each of these forms of expression is making clear (as we have noted in Chapter 7) is that love for God requires the whole person – mind, feelings, and will, with all their energy. It is a reaching out and committing oneself on the part of the whole person.

Loving another human being is the same. It too involves reaching out in commitment to someone else, reaching out with affection and consideration, reaching out by thinking of them and seeking to understand them and thinking the best of them, reaching out by spending time and money and energy and life. It involves the whole person given to someone else. That is how God's love for us is : it involves God's thinking and affection and acting. God thinks the best of us, wants to understand us and likes to hear us talk in order to develop that process. God feels warm about us, smiles at us and laughs at us with the laugh of the lover whose smile is an expression of affection, not the laugh of the scorner whose smile implies superiority or disdain. God gives everything for us, even the only son God had.

(ii)

Love is thus a demanding business, even a painful business. The feeling in the pit of the stomach is as likely to be an anxious pain as an excited flutter. That is true of romantic love, but also of other forms of love. The point is well expressed in Hannah Hurnard's allegory of love, *Hinds' Feet on High Places* (CMJ, 1955). The hero, Much-Afraid, shrinks back from having the seed of Love planted in her heart. 'I am afraid. . . . I have been told that if you really love someone you give that loved one the power to hurt and pain you in a way nothing else can.' The Shepherd's response is to affirm the truth of that, but to add that there is happiness in love even if you are not loved in return. Yet he promised that when Love was ready to bloom in her heart and when she was ready to change her name, she would in fact be loved in return. And he offered her the seed of Love.

> She bent forward to look, then gave a startled little cry and drew back. There was indeed a seed . . . but it was shaped exactly like a long, sharply pointed thorn. Much-Afraid had often noticed that the Shepherd's hands were scarred and wounded, but now she saw that the scar in the palm of the hand held out to her was the exact shape and size of the seed of Love lying beside it.

The Shepherd reminded her that 'Love and Pain go together, for a time at least. If you would know Love, you must know pain too' (pp. 16–17).

It is not a uniquely Christian insight. Richard Olivier comments in *Shadow of the Stone Heart*, to which I referred in Chapter 9, 'I was learning the hard way you can't just increase the capacity to love without simultaneously increasing the propensity for pain' (p. 160). But he was determined that he would no longer sacrifice the feelings of love and joy because they involved owning the feelings of pain and loss; 'As someone once said, "It is important that when Death finds you, it finds you alive" ' (p. 182).

It is easy for love to be self-centred, to be at least as much interested in the love we get in return for giving love as in the mere giving of the love itself (we are back to the Adversary's question in Job). Real love gains its happiness from the giving, not the anticipated or actual reciprocating. It is a little like artistic creativity. The painter or sculptor or musician may not care whether anyone appreciates their work; that is not the point. The point is to have created something true.

So it is with love. Its point is to have done something true, even if the object of love makes no response, even can make no response. (Of course we know that there is a response of love from God, whose heart thrills with delight and loves us so much because we have loved.)

In due course Much-Afraid reaches an exalted place, dominated by a mighty waterfall, whose waters leap down from a height high above her and her two companions Sorrow and Suffering. The Shepherd asks Much-Afraid:

'What do you think of this fall of great waters in their abandonment of self-giving?' She trembled a little as she answered, 'I think they are beautiful and terrible beyond anything which I ever saw before.' 'Why terrible?' he asked. 'It is the leap which they have to make, the awful height from which they must cast themselves down to the depths beneath, there to be broken on the rocks. I can hardly bear to watch it.' 'Look closer,' he said again. 'Let your eye follow just one part of the water from the moment when it leaps over the edge until it reaches the bottom.' Much-Afraid did so, and then almost gasped with wonder. Once over the edge, the waters were like winged things, alive with joy, so utterly abandoned to the ecstasy of giving themselves that she could almost have supposed that she was looking at a host of angels floating down on rainbow wings, singing with rapture as they went. She gazed and gazed, then said, 'It looks as though they think it is the loveliest moment in all the world, as though to cast oneself down is to abandon oneself to ecstasy and joy indescribable.' . . . The lower the water fell, the lighter it seemed to grow, as though it really were lighting down on wings. On reaching the rocks below, all the waters flowed together in a glorious host, forming an exuberant, rushing torrent which swirled triumphantly around and over the rocks. Laughing and shouting at the top of their voices, they hurried still lower and lower, down through the meadows to the next precipice and the next glorious crisis of their self-giving. (pp. 115–6)

(iii)

'There is nothing love cannot face; there is no limit to its faith, is hope, and its endurance': so the NEB's version of 1 Corinthians 13:7. It is tempting to think that there are many things that love cannot face. When you have done something wrong by someone you love, you may naturally and rightly fear telling them. You are not sure their love can face it. We once knew a woman who had had an abortion some years ago. She had never told any of the friends she had made since she had come to faith in Christ, because she feared that this would destroy their picture of her (or their love for her) as the joyful dedicated Christian she is.

God's love can face things. I was tempted to suggest that this was just as well, because God has difficulty avoiding knowing things, but then I recalled that God has more control of remembering and forgetting than we do, so presumably God can avoid knowing things (even though we cannot avoid God knowing things if God chooses to!). But if our relationship with God were based on God not knowing some things about us, that would imperil the relationship. It would make it unreal. The more committed a relationship is, the more important it seems that we should be able to say anything in its context, and in particular that we should be able to share the shameful things. Otherwise, apparent depth in the relationship turns out to be based on falsehood. If there is real love in the relationship, we need to be able to take the initiative and share shameful things, and then (perhaps) have the experience of these things not seeming anywhere near as shameful to the other person as they seem to us, or the experience of having them say that they had guessed that there was something like this in the background anyway, and that it does not matter. God is like that; God's love can face things. Worthwhile love on the part of other human beings is like that too; their love can face things. And for us to love involves being instinctively like that ourselves. We can face things in other people, and thereby bring them a new form of freedom as they can bring shameful things out of the cupboard and find that in the daylight of love they pale into insignificance.

There is no limit to love's faith, to its capacity to believe in the other person. God demonstrated an extraordinary faith in Israel and in what it could be and achieve, like the belief a mother has in her children or a wife has in her husband. Indeed, both the analogy of parenthood and that of marriage appear in Israel's story. Then Jesus tells eleven members of Israel that he is entrusting them with the task of discipling all the nations. There is a midrash which has Jesus announcing this plan to the angels ahead of time. One of them asks what is his plan if this one fails. 'I have no other plan,' he says. That is the degree of his faith in them, his trust in them. Our love for each other involves a similar trust, a belief in the other person which may make it possible for them to do things which they could not otherwise do because they do not believe in themselves as much as we do.

That overlaps with the significance of the fact that there is no limit to love's hope. God had a vision for Israel, the way a mother has a vision for her children. The story in Hosea 11 draws painful attention to the way a mother's vision may be long unfulfilled, but it is not abandoned. God has a vision for us, and is not yet finished with us. That is a powerful stimulus to change for us. And we have a vision for people we love. It is an old joke that when a woman marries a man, she is convinced that she will change him. But there is a difference between having a vision of what we wish another person to be and having a vision of what they could be, a vision which sees the realization of potentials we can perhaps see in them. We may be able to hope for them what they could not hope for themselves. There is no limit to love's hope.

And there is no limit to its endurance. Again, we can see that this is so as we consider the story of God's relationship with Israel, or with the church. And again the comparison with a mother is an instructive one. The picture in Hosea 11 presupposes that a mother's endurance is never exhausted. My Old Testament colleague who is a mother talks about the fact that no matter what her sons do, no matter how exasperated or angry with them she might become, she could never cease being their mother. She in one sense looks forward to the time when they will grow up and leave home to live their lives as adults, but she could never throw them out because they had finally crossed some line. There is no limit to the endurance of a mother's love. Perhaps women are better at facing and trusting and hoping and enduring. Our love for each other will persist.

As the time of our departure from England drew near, I went to a farewell lunch with some of our students. Towards the end one delivered a touching speech. 'You have too big a love for St John's College,' he said, 'and I am afraid that your love will be too big for Fuller Seminary.' I did not know what he meant, but it sounded a very nice thing to say, and I wanted to think about it and wonder whether it was some form of word from God. Then I realized that actually he had said, 'You have too big a laugh for St John's College, and I am afraid your laugh will be too big for Fuller Seminary.'

But the notions of a 'big love' and of 'too big a love' bear thinking about. It is a big love that can face anything and that has no end to its faith, its hope, and its endurance. And too big a love overflows and spills out to others. It does not make the mistake that Ann and I may have made without realizing it, which I described at the beginning of Chapter 7. It makes a love-relationship something open and overflowing, not a closed '*egoïsme de deux*' (a piece of selfishness on the part of two people).

(iv)

For his book on religion and rock, Steve Turner took his title from Bruce Springsteen's song 'Hungry For Heaven'. Turner's thesis is that the restlessness expressed in rock music and usually focused on human relationships is the same restlessness that Augustine speaks of, one which reaches out further than it realizes. The live version of 'Hungry Heart' on Springsteen's retrospective compilation of live performances shows why music is a live business: he leaves the audience quite alone to do the singing at the beginning. (A gig is somewhat like church: people know why they are there, it is a communal event, they know the words, and they don't need to be told the page number.)

Springsteen sings the story of someone who has kept seeking the fulfilment of his heart's longing and in the course of doing that has gone in for a few betrayals but never finds a place to rest, a home. 'Everybody's got a hungry heart.'

As happened with 'Many Rivers to Cross', I was once struck by a few lines of a track on Jeff Buckley's album *Grace*, which also made me try to grasp the whole. It shattered me when I did. This time it is the story of a Bible character, David, a man with much more ambiguity in his life than the plaster saint portrayals usually allow. In the song David is the baffled king, singing hallelujah but no longer understanding God, beguiled by a woman and letting her break his throne in return for the joy she brought him, proving that love is 'a cold and . . . a broken hallelujah'.

The lines simultaneously and devastatingly question the reality of human relationships and of relationships with God (as well as the significance of music) and thus bring out into the open the secret dreads and doubts about God and other loves which we dare not name even to ourselves. And the fact that they do this to both at the same time means that we can neither escape from the doubted God to a human love nor escape from a doubted human love to God.

The song is by Leonard Cohen, the Canadian Jewish writer and composer who often takes up religious themes in such as way as this, though nowhere else as disturbingly, I would say. Jennifer Warnes, who was once a backing singer for Cohen and who has herself recorded an album of his songs, said of Cohen that the great thing about him was that he said the things that no one else would say. At the hands of Leonard Cohen, the implicit reaching out of 'Hungry Heart' deconstructs.

In spring 1997 Jeff Buckley, who had made the definitive recording of this song, walked into the Mississippi and drowned, dragged into an undertow by a riverboat. First accounts said he was playing his guitar, which seemed bizarre. A later version reported more plausibly that as he went in for a swim he was singing to Led Zeppelin's 'Whole Lotta Love' as it played on a ghetto-blaster. He was just past the age when his singer father, Tim Buckley, whom he never met, died of drugs.

I have suggested that Meat Loaf's 'Bat Out Of Hell' (itself a love song) illustrates how Jim Steinman's songs and arrangements are written as if for fun, but deceive you because they often conceal a sting or a sadness in the tale/tail. My next favourite to 'Bat Out of Hell' is 'Two Out of Three Ain't Bad': I need you, I want you, but there ain't no way I'm ever going to love you. It sounds stereotypically male. But then as you listen to the song it turns out that he cannot let himself love because of his experience of being broken by the woman who he thought loved him and who said those words to him. Which is the stereotypical male theme which dominates rock, really.

My favourite film of 1995 was *Leaving Las Vegas*, the story of an alcoholic writer who goes to Las Vegas to drink himself to death. There he meets a prostitute and they fall in love. It means that he dies loved, while she goes into the rest of her life having loved. Someone who came to see it with Ann and me was puzzled as to why a Christian wanted to see such a gloomy film. For me it was an encouraging film because it looked the grimmest of experiences in the eye and declared that if there was love, it was possible to die and it was also possible to live on (better to have loved and lost . . .).

About the same time we went to see *Sense and Sensibility* towards which I have a certain antipathy. The story involves the threat that two women would lose the men they loved. Twenty minutes before the end I thought and hoped it was going to turn out like that, with the two sisters then proving that it was possible to live on with each other's sisterly friendship. But in those last few minutes everything got sorted out and the sisters were able to marry happily.

We were discussing the two films with friends and I was saying how much I preferred *Leaving Las Vegas*. One of the friends who knew me too well commented, 'Yes, you would go for doomed romance.' I protested that it was romanced doom that I went for (i.e. gloom tempered by romance), but later I realized that the

comment was right. I like the idea suggested by *Leaving Las Vegas*
that even if love is doomed and it is necessary to live on anyway,
this can be possible. But I can only believe that because God is
real and Leonard Cohen's awful vision can therefore be looked in
the face but not seen as the final word.

13

Realism

(i) Facing the facts as an individual

Jesus once told an extraordinary story about a farm manager. The farm owner had given him a formal warning about being dissatisfied with his work performance. This galvanized him into action, which rather shows that he need never have got into this mess. He summoned the owner's creditors and told them that if they paid now, he would settle for half the amount they owed. At least that would mean he had 'friends' when he lost his job. When the owner discovered what had happened, he was unable to conceal his admiration for the manager's shrewdness.

If you know the British television series *Minder*, you will be able to translate Jesus' parable into the plot for an episode. Arthur Daly decides to make Terry redundant. In the series Arthur is actually the shady character and Terry, his minder, gofer, and general dogsbody, is nearer than most people to a man of honour. But one can quite imagine Arthur receiving at least trumped-up complaints about Terry, which it is in his interest to take seriously because business is slack, and he cannot really afford Terry's wages. So Terry loses his job. What is he to do? If he has no job, he has no wages. If he has no wages, he has no flat. How will he survive?

In the parable the manager, like many managers, is really only a penpusher. Terry is not like that. He is actually quite strong enough to dig, and he is not as proud as his boss – though part of the irony of the series, as I have hinted already, is that as a human being he really has more to be proud of. Perhaps Terry might say to himself: 'I'm not clever enough to get a desk job. I'm too suspect in the eyes of the law to be taken on by lots of firms. How can I get on the right side of some people, so that they'll bail me out, give me a sofa to sleep on, maybe even some casual work?'

So Terry goes straight off to see some of Arthur's creditors, the sort of people he is usually expected to apply a little friendly pressure to when Arthur himself is under pressure and needs some ready cash. Terry tells them that as a special gesture of Christmas goodwill Arthur is cutting their debts in half. They can hardly believe it. They are well aware that Arthur does not know the meaning of the phrase 'Christmas goodwill', unless it is the name of a horse running in the 2.30 at Kempton Park. But in a situation like that, who is going to ask any inquisitive questions? They are going to take the money, or rather sign the cheque, and run.

The result is that they all think that Terry is wonderful. He therefore has friends for when he needs them when he is out of a job, and they also all think Arthur is wonderful for being so generous. The word soon reaches the Worthington, their pub, and Arthur Daly is the toast of South London. You can just see him looking simultaneously flattered, pleased, puzzled and suspicious, as people congratulate him on his magnificent gesture.

When he discovers what has been going on, he has to congratulate Terry for his shrewdness, does he not? He cannot go back on the deal because he would lose so much face and no longer be the local hero. Indeed, he cannot really be that displeased, in the circumstances. Terry's investment at Arthur's expense has brought profit to Arthur as well as to Terry. Brilliant! Roll the credits, play the theme music.

There is an organization called the Scripture Union which among other things publishes notes to help people understand the Bible. The organization has a logo consisting of an oil lamp, recalling the verse in the Psalms that describes God's word as a lamp to illuminate the way for us. Years ago I heard someone suggest that if the logo was ever redesigned it ought to be changed into a pair of raised eyebrows, because the Bible is always saying things that surprise us. It is never predictable or boring. The parables are best of all at such surprises. In another parable a widow makes a terrible nuisance of herself at the private residence of a judge, who eventually sees that justice is done only because this is the only way he can get the wretched woman off his back. And that is an example of prayer. Then there is the one about the Publican and the Pharisee going to church. Think of the Publican as an embodiment of the Thatcherite enterprise economy; think of the Pharisee as a the committed churchman, concerned to see the scriptures embodied in his own life and other people's – think of him as a theological college principal, perhaps. Who goes home right with God? Not the theological college principal. Or what about the man who gets mugged on the way to Jericho, and ignored by another principal, and by a hospital chaplain, but gets cared for by – well, who is equivalent to a Samaritan? The local National Front Secretary? A Muslim fundamentalist looking forward to burning Salman Rushdie when he finds him?

Why are Jesus' parables so extraordinary, so eyebrow-raising? There are various reasons, but what lies behind them is the fact that the gospel that Jesus is and that he brings is so important but so extraordinary that it needs eyebrow-raising stories to convey it; it needs shock tactics to get it taken seriously. Jesus told the story of the shrewd manager to try to shake people out of torpor into action.

The reason was that Jesus put people into a position in which key decisions had to be taken. He knew he came from God. His coming meant that the crucial moment in his people's history was dawning – indeed, the crucial moment in world history was dawning. He had come to bring new life to Israel, and new life to the world. What attitude people took to Jesus would make a decisive difference to their whole destiny. The question was, could they recognize that the decisive moment had arrived, that their number was up?

There are moments like that for governments. Indeed, there are quite close parallels between party politics and the shrewd manager: does not his story also remind you of some chancellor of the exchequer distributing largesse on the eve of an election, in the conviction that that is the way to buy re-election from the voters?

There are also moments like that in our personal lives. This is one of the themes in the film *Dead Poets Society*, a marvellous if rather pagan story about young men discovering who they are, and becoming willing to be different and not to conform to the expectations of parents and other despised species. One of them accidentally meets the girl of his dreams and in order to woo her has to take action that is dangerously and amusingly bold, given that she is already nearly engaged to a large football-playing gentleman. Another throws himself into acting despite his father's insistence that the boy is destined to be a doctor. They cannot let life simply wash over them, if they are to become someone and to do what they have to do. They have to take decisions, to take action.

Just after our parable Luke tells us of some words of Jesus that comprise a challenge to a decision. 'No one can serve two masters' (Luke 16:13). You have to choose between God and Mammon. I am about to move to a post that pays twice as much as my present one. What will serving Christ mean now? How will I live with money and God? How does one use worldly wealth in a way that brings us nearer an eternal home (Luke 16:9)? Many people no doubt wish that was their problem, instead of the problem of making ends meet. But all of us have to face a decision regarding God or Mammon, a broad gate or a narrow one through which we need to walk if we are to join the few who find life. It does not happen accidentally. It does not happen if you simply drift. That, says Jesus, is the broad way which leads nowhere or worse.

Jesus did not just bring a crisis and a challenge to a decision to first-century people, scribes and fishermen and zealots and whores and priests and tax collectors and other characters quite unlike us. He was the decisive person in world history, and he still is. 'Don't be so stupid that you fail to recognize a decisive moment when it arrives,' says Jesus. 'Don't be like Arthur. Be like Terry.'

(ii) Facing the facts as a community

The date is 17 October, the year 520 BC. It is the last day of the Feast of Tabernacles, Israel's great festival at the end of the farming year in the autumn, one of the occasions when people came to Jerusalem on pilgrimage. The occasion was a cross between Christmas or Easter and Spring Harvest or Keswick or Greenbelt. People camped together for a week and looked back over what God had done for them and wondered what the new year would bring.

There is a special significance about this particular year in the history of the people of God, and God sends Haggai to them with a special message, recorded in Haggai 2:1–9. Like a typical prophet Haggai points the people to some facts about past, present, and future in order to bring them promises and challenges.

He wants them to face the real facts about the past. At the Feast of Tabernacles they might be able to avoid facing these facts. It almost encouraged them to do that. After all, the festival was designed to remind them of the wonder of God's deliverance of them from Egypt, when they had to camp on the way. If they were having a great celebration of God's acts, they might be averting their eyes from the realities of the more recent past. On the other hand, the reminder of those acts of God might mean they could hardly avoid the contrast between the Exodus story and their own more recent past and present.

Haggai gently draws attention to the contrast between past and present and invites them to own it. He reminds them of the fact that their days of glory lie in the past. There was once a day when Davidic kings ruled in Jerusalem. They had real kings then – all they have now is Zerubbabel the son of Shealtiel. His genealogy marks him as a person who could be king if there was a king, but all in all he is a 'governor' appointed by the Persians.

There was once a day when they had quality high priests, people whose position no one would query. All they have now is Joshua the son of Jehozadak, and we know from Zechariah 3 that he was disparaged (by members of the local population who had not been into exile) as being tainted by the impurity of exile.

There was once a day when they were a real people, an entity to be reckoned with in Middle Eastern politics and history. All they are now is a 'remnant'. We know what a remnant is – it is the left-over bits of wallpaper or material that a shop sells off cheaply.

Haggai particularly notes that they had a real temple then, one which puts to shame the temple the community is trying to build. This new temple is really less than nothing. Its shape may be the same (the First Temple was not demolished), but it has lost the covenant chest and the covenant stones, the cherubim, the pot of manna, Aaron's rod, the urim and thummim, the imported wooden panelling, the gold . . . People who were old enough to have known the First Temple (they would have had to be over 70!) wept when they saw the Second (see Ezra 3: Ezra 1–6 tells the story, that is, the context for the work of Haggai and Zechariah).

Facing facts is difficult. That is true about individuals: doctors and relatives find it hard to tell someone they have a terminal disease. It is true about a nation: a country such as Britain finds it difficult to come to terms with its reduced significance in the world. It is true about the church: it is tempting to hide from the fact that the church is in decline. How can you face facts?

Haggai believes that the key is to consider the invisible facts about the present. In his first prophecy he was rather confrontational in rebuking them about their commitment to God. Here he wants to be encouraging. The invisible facts about the present are what makes it possible to face the real facts about the past.

'I am with you – be strong, says Yahweh Sebaot.' That phrase is Haggai's special title for God. English translations have 'the LORD Almighty', which waters it down. The name means 'Yahweh Armies'. It expresses concretely and vividly the power of God, which is what the people need to believe in. They are merely 'people of the land' – ordinary people without great resources or status. God's nature as Yahweh Armies contrasts with theirs and opens up the possibility of facing those other facts.

'My spirit remains among you. Do not be afraid. Remember how it was when I brought you out of Egypt.' This theme will fit the Feast of Tabernacles. The Exodus will be a bitter-sweet memory because of the contrast with present experience. Haggai offers them some alternative facts about the past to set against those about the present.

The hidden facts about God in the present provide a context in which we face facts about an individual's illness, or about a nation which has lost an empire and not found a role, or about a church in decline. Hope lies not in doctrinal soundness or trendiness or social involvement or the latest charisms. Haggai's encouragement is God. The resource of the church is God active in a hidden way building up the people of God as a temple of the Spirit.

As well as facing the facts about the past and the hidden facts about the present, Haggai wants them to look at the guaranteed facts about the future. Faith means being sure of what we hope for and certain of what we do not see (Hebrews 11:1). 'I will fill this house with glory,' God says. The recurrent word in Haggai's vision of their future is 'glory'. Glory suggests the outward visible splendour of a monarch in state robes. It is not the nature of their own recent or present experience.

For Israel it will mean 'prosperity' (RSV) or 'peace' (NIV): both aspects of the meaning of '*shalom*' are surely appropriate (REB). Yet what Haggai promises will come about for God's glory not merely for Israel's sake. All the world will come to worship at the throne of the king.

It will come about by God's act – it was God who filled the temple with glory before, and it will be God who does so again. Human beings cannot make that happen. Hence it can be promised as coming 'in a little while'. It is imminent because it is only dependent on God's acting, on God's shaking.

It will come about as part of a final reordering of all things. It will involve a great 'shaking' like the shaking at the Exodus and Sinai (cf. Hebrews 12:25–27). Zechariah also grieved at the fact that in his and Haggai's day all seemed peace and quiet. He knew that when God acted there had to be upheaval. That was promise not threat.

As with many promises and threats in scripture, the final reordering did not come in the prophet's day, but something did, a kind of foretaste of the final fulfilment of God's promise (see Ezra 6 regarding how things turned out). So it often is with healing and with peace among the nations and with renewal in the church.

We have to ask for them as gifts that belong to the End. They will only become full reality in connection with the End. But we have to look for the little foretastes which may be what we ourselves get in the meantime, and rejoice in these for what they are and for what they themselves promise.

The facts about the future are guaranteed by the word of Yahweh Armies, Almighty God (eight times in Haggai 2:6–9). When God speaks, things will happen.

(iii) Limitations

I expect some Israelites thought the same about Ecclesiastes as the students whom I mentioned in Chapter 2 did about me and U2. I love Ecclesiastes. Well, actually I love all the Old Testament. I have friends who belong to the New Testament Church of God. I always say I belong to the Old Testament Church of God. One of the things I love about it is the way it interacts with our human life as it is. And the book that does that most systematically is Ecclesiastes.

The name is Greek; it means 'church member' or 'church leader'. That corresponds to the book's Hebrew name, Qohelet, which has the same meaning. The opening verse of the book thus describes what follows as the words of the 'teacher' or 'preacher'. It then identifies him as the son of David and king in Jerusalem, which enhances the book's authority, because it means this is a book of wisdom like the Proverbs 'of Solomon' or the Song of Songs 'of Solomon'.

After that it may be surprising to find that the opening words of Solomon's teaching are 'Meaningless! Meaningless! Utterly meaningless! Everything is meaningless!' It turns out that there is another significance in the opening verse putting us in mind of Solomon. Because Solomon was the man who had everything. So if there was ever a man who had the chance to find what he was looking for, it was Solomon.

Solomon stands for the use of the mind; but he acknowledges that the more he has discovered intellectually, the more grief he has felt. He has asked many questions, but not found many answers. Solomon stands for enjoyment, but his story shows that it turned to dust in his mouth. Solomon stands for achievement: he is the man who built the temple and made Jerusalem what it was. But that has turned into dust in his mouth as well. It is meaningless. The word literally means a breath.

Christians are inclined to stand superior in relation to Ecclesiastes. It may seem to resemble the darkness into which the gospel in due course will shine more than the light of the gospel itself. Yet when we talk this way we may be hiding from the reality of how Christian life is. For Christians work at intellectual questions such as the meaning of suffering, and do not know the answers. Christians try to get to the top of the ladder in their profession, try to win architectural competitions and to get into the final at Wimbledon and to make a hit album and to get elected to parliament. And some succeed. And they find that these achievements turn to dust in their mouths.

Indeed there is more. In a telling observation the Teacher describes how 'God has made everything beautiful in its time, and has also set eternity in the human heart; yet they cannot fathom what God has done from beginning to end' (3:11). That has not changed. And the problem is not merely intellectual. The Teacher has seen something else. Where there ought to be just judgment, actually there is wickedness (3:16). The teacher has seen the oppression that takes place in the world (another irony here, for the historical Solomon was a major cause of it in his own country):

> I saw the tears of the oppressed –
> and they have no comforter;
> power was on the side of their oppressors –
> and they have no comforter. (4:1)

Page after page of this realism confronts us, rubbing our nose in the realities of human experience which affect believers as they do unbelievers.

'Solomon's' conclusion is then surprising. It is that people can do nothing better than to eat and drink and find satisfaction in their work. That comes from God. It is God's gift (3:22).

A portrait of God as the great giver is the surprising centre to the theology of Ecclesiastes. We feel a huge tension between the exposure of all pretension to understand or make sense of life and the bold and stark invitation to hold faith in God the giver, but it sets before us a vision preferable to the alternatives. For what are these alternatives? To pretend that the question is not there and that everything can be seen to be solved in Christ? That is the usual Christian ploy. To pretend that the question is not there and that we can find meaning in fame or achievement or whatever? That is the usual non-Christian ploy. I prefer Ecclesiastes' invitation to realism and trust.

14

Remembering

When Moses is about to give up the leadership of Israel, as the Old Testament tells the story, he preaches one last sermon. He has led them for a generation and they are now to pass on to a new stage of their life, and God has made it clear that this new stage and this seeing the fulfilment of God's vision is to happen under a different leader. He can look on into the land where God's vision is taking them, he knows what it looks like, but he will not walk in it with them. He is about to undertake a new journey of his own, the first time for forty years that he will be journeying with God apart from them, and the mountain he is about to climb has some surprises in store for him.

So on the eve of his climbing his mountain, he preaches a sermon. It is a long one, this book Deuteronomy. I calculate that the actual sermon is about 25,000 words, which would take four hours to preach non-stop. When you preach your last sermon in circumstances like Moses', what do you say? What did the Deuteronomists (the anonymous religious visionaries who ghosted this sermon some centuries later, on the usual critical view) think Moses would have wanted people to remember? From all those words I take four motifs from 7:6–11.

First, remember that you are a holy people. In the Old Testament the word 'holy' does not mean righteous and moral. It means special to God, different, awe-inspiring. You are a special, different, awe-inspiring people, says Moses. It is a position that belongs to Israel, and which the church then comes to share in without replacing Israel. 'You are a people holy to Yahweh your God.'

Being holy meant having nothing to do with the way the Canaanites were. After all, 'Yahweh your God chose you out of all nations on earth to be his special possession.' The Israelites resembled the rooms in Buckingham Palace that you do not see when you go on the tour, the rooms that belong especially to the queen. They had that specialness to Yahweh. They were to be different. Israel never took any notice of this expectation, and we do not want to be different either. Forty years ago Christians were different: we did not go to the pub or the cinema or go dancing, for instance, or if we did, we knew we were breaking taboos. Now we are all indistinguishable from the world, and it is not obviously a step forward. Yet I do not really want Christians to start looking different in that kind of way.

So how should we be different? What is holiness? When you think about it, to call human beings holy is a kind of contradiction in terms. 'Holy' is by definition what makes God God and what distinguishes God from us. So what sense does it make to call us holy?

I wonder whether for us being holy means being supernaturally human. It means being human, but in a way that is redolent of God, that is special, that is supernatural. The way Ann and I have to be holy is by coping with Ann's illness. The way anyone else has to be holy will be different. But as I think of the Christians whom I know best, I think of them being human, but of there being something special, something supernatural about them in their humanness.

There is a British television programme called *How do they do that?* (for instance, how do they make certain 'tricks' work in television advertisements?) That is what I think of many of my Christian friends. How does he do that? How does she manage to be that kind of person? It is probably something they are unconscious of, or take for granted, but for other people it is what makes them special, what makes them holy. I do not think much about the heroics of coping with a wife who is disabled, and I am always a bit astonished when someone else comments on the patience it needs or on some other aspects of how Ann and I handle Ann's illness. I know that people find it is something through which God gets access to us in some mysterious way. And that is true of aspects of who other people are, too. It is as we let the people we are be the people we are with God that the supernatural appears through the human and the world has the opportunity to see that there is something different about us. That is something I would want to leave with people if I were going, like Moses.

But Moses is talking corporately. It is as the people of God that he reminds them they are holy. I want to encourage belief in the church as God's holy people.

Each summer at college we have a day to which we invite the vicars who are receiving curates from us, so that they can see something of the training from which their curates are coming. One year I was appalled at the paternalism that emerged in the way some of the vicars spoke of their congregations. They felt that it was important that the vicar and the curate decide on their line about policy issues before the church council discussed them, otherwise it would be confusing for the people, would it not? Who do they think are the holy people of God? The clergy are simply paid functionaries whose position puts them in greater spiritual danger than anyone else in the church. It is the church that is in holy orders, by virtue of our baptism. To put it in Deuteronomy's terms, the declaration that God chose Israel comes before any talk of God's choosing the king. The people were familiar with the idea that God chose David. The Deuteronomists dared to preface it with the declaration that the choice of David, like the choice of the priesthood, was subordinate to the choosing of the whole people.

And Moses is inviting his hearers to believe in the holiness of the actual Israel, the visible church if you like, the actual church which exists, the Church of England and the Methodist Connexion and the Baptist Union and the Korean Presbyterian Church and the Church of God (Cleveland, Tennessee) and the Coptic Orthodox Church. It is always tempting to redefine the church to mean the group we belong to, the bit of the church that we think is alive. It is tempting to be cynical about the church that actually exists, as comes out in our jokes. When Moses says 'you are a holy people', he is talking about the Israel that actually exists. It is the visible church that is holy, and therefore it is not to be dismissed or despaired of. Remember that you are a holy people.

Second, remember that you are loved. In Chapter 7 I suggested that it is better, if you have the choice, to fall in love with your friends than to try to make friends of your lovers. Moses here implies that this was what God did. He uses two words for love. 'It was not because you were more numerous than any other nation that Yahweh cared for you and chose you.' 'Cared for you.' 'Set his affection on you', the NIV has. 'How did Yahweh come to have those feelings for you, come to be attached to you?' asks Moses: it is a word that can describe people's sexual feelings for each other. 'Well, it was not because there were so many of you,' he answers. This is just as well. When the Deuteronomists were writing this sermon, Israel's heyday lay in the past, and it would be as well if the reason Yahweh was attached to them was not that there were so many of them, and this is as well for us, too.

Perhaps it is the ecclesiological equivalent of 'Will you still need me, will you still feed me, when I am 64?' 'When my hair is gone and I can't stay up as late as I once did, when I've gone pear-shaped and cellulite, will you still love me?' 'It was not things about how you looked that made me love you in the first place, fathead.' 'So why did you love me?'

At this point, if you've got Nora Ephron as your scriptwriter, you say as Harry did to Sally, 'I love that you get cold when it is 71 degrees out. I love that it takes you an hour and a half to order a sandwich. I love that you get a little crinkle above your nose when you're looking at me as though I'm nuts. I love that when I've been with you all day I can still smell your perfume on my clothes. And I love that you are the last person I want to talk to before I go to sleep at night.' (Having sent off all my CDs with the rest of our belongings ahead of us to the USA, I have been reduced to watching videos at night, but at least it means I am watching my favourite films before I have to consign them to the dustbin of the Cisatlantic video system.) If you have Hosea as your scriptwriter, it is the same. You say things like, 'When I found Israel, it was like finding grapes in the desert.'

But if you are just an ordinary prosaic British person, when you get asked, 'So why do you love me?' you get lost for words and perhaps you simply say, 'I just did, and I still do.' So it is when the Deuteronomists are writing Yahweh's script. Moses moves to the other word for love, the all-purpose Hebrew word that can still mean affection and passion but can also suggest friendship and commitment. 'I did not get attached to you because there were so many of you. It was just because I loved you. I found myself committed to you and I could not get out of it. It had become part of me. I had to do what I'd told Abraham and Sarah I would do.'

Remember you are loved: that God is attached to you and committed to you, for reasons to do with you maybe, but certainly for reasons to do with God. No matter what seems to happen to the church, God loves it and will continue to be committed to it. It means God has not finished with it. God will fulfil the promises made to it.

Third, remember that you are called to knowledge. As I come to the end of ten years as principal of an Anglican theological college, I have from time to time wondered what it has been about. When I had just been appointed principal, there was an informal chapel occasion which ended up with the teaching staff who were present out in the front and someone praying for us and giving each of us a word from God. I have already mentioned mine, that I had had a vision for the college and I had not thought it would be fulfilled, but that it would be fulfilled.

I thought this referred to the college becoming more relaxed about charismatic gifts, and more open, and that has happened, but I have come to realize something else. Sometimes you only know what a prophecy meant when it has been fulfilled, and over the past two or three years I think we have seen a quantum leap in our integration of theology and prayer and life. That was always my subconscious vision, but I did not have much hope that these could ever come together. I did not even articulate that vision, but God had it and shared it and it has come about. I believed that people were called to knowledge.

'Know then that Yahweh your God is God,' says Moses, and adds some further theological facts about Yahweh that the people are to know. It sounds like the essence of doing theology, and it is. But the NRSV rightly translates it as 'acknowledging' these facts about Yahweh, not just knowing them. It assumes that theology and commitment are one thing, not two things. That is something Moses wants to leave with people when he goes. When theological students are in the classroom they are not playing academic games. They are worshipping. And when they are in chapel, they are not playing religious games. They are knowing.

What are those facts about God? For Moses the key one is that God is faithful, someone who keeps covenant and commitment. 'Know then that Yahweh your God is God, the faithful God.'

I am glad about that because I feel in special need of it. I am leaving because God made it clear that the moment had come. We are going where we are going not so much because God guided as because God pushed and manipulated. People ask me from time to time if I am excited about it, and the answer is 'Not especially'. It is just the direction God has pushed us. People say it is courageous; it would have required more courage to stay here. But all sorts of things could go wrong. There was a time when we had sent our belongings off but had not actually completed purchase on the apartment we had sent them to, nor had we got a mortgage, and a package about that had gone astray in the post. We had not got a visa, and the embassy phone lines were permanently busy. Just before we left we heard that our belongings were not going to be there before us, as we had planned, and I am not sure how we will work around that. I expect it will be OK; but there are other more personal things that could go wrong, and I have to trust (more of that in Chapter 19) that it is true that God is faithful.

Moses offers us various encouragements. He reminds us that Yahweh has been faithful in the past, keeping that promise to

Abraham and Sarah. He reminds us that Yahweh bothered to exercise divine power and bothered to deliver us into the freedom we already enjoy even when we are not actually in a promised land, so surely the wilderness will not be the end. He reminds us that there is a vast disparity between God's responsiveness to lovers and to haters. Punishment for the haters, yes; but faithfulness to a thousand generations for the lovers. One generation will do, thank you. For us, I am at least encouraged by the signs that it is indeed God who is doing the pushing and manipulating, so that if we end up in a mess and I feel, as I sometimes do, that God could have made my life a bit easier, well, at least I will know that I am in this hole with God. We have to remember that we are called to knowledge, knowledge of the God who is faithful.

Fourth, remember that you are called to follow God's word. What Moses says more specifically is, 'You are to observe these commandments, statutes and laws which I give you this day, and keep them.' I do not actually like that. I do not see why God is so keen on giving commandments. I am not very keen on giving commands – why is God? I do not want people to obey me – why does God? I cannot believe that if I were God I would be so keen on issuing orders. It seems such an odd thing to enjoy, even if you do know best.

So at the moment this is an angle on scripture that I am trying to wrestle with. Other people will have other questions about scripture. If there are no aspects of scripture that they do not like and do not have to wrestle with, then they are kidding themselves. It means that they have bracketed them out or reinterpreted them. That is what as evangelicals we have to do. We know we have to accept all of scripture, so we make it mean something else so we can accept it. As a Bible teacher one of my basic concerns has become simply to get people to read the Bible with open eyes. Some people learn to, others do not. I want people to read the Bible, to be open to finding there things that they had not realized were there, to be enthralled and dazzled and appalled and infuriated and puzzled and worried and stimulated and kept awake at night by these extraordinary words from God, to let their mind and heart and imagination and will be provoked and astonished by them. I want them to 'observe them . . . and keep them'.

If Moses and Israel will commit themselves to that, together and apart, they can cross their river, and he can climb his mountain.

15

Repentance

(i)

According to Psalm 32, confession is good for you. You find relief, forgiveness, protection, guidance, and a joy like heaven's own.

As human beings we are all in the condemning and criticizing business (parents-teachers, vicars-congregations, police-community . . .). Perhaps this is partly because inside we feel condemned ourselves. Traditionally the church has been thought to have a particular preoccupation with sexual sin, despite the wonderful story in John 8 which subverts any such preoccupation. It is a story of a woman who has indeed gone wrong sexually, though we are not in a position to assess degrees of blameworthiness; indeed to do so would be to subvert the point of the story. The woman would be condemned by society, and specifically by religious society, as Aids victims are in ours. And we assume that God shares the condemning or criticizing attitude.

But we also know that God is not in the condemning business. The cross is the demonstration of that. But this story shows it. First, Jesus denies being in the condemning business. Second, he therefore tells the woman she can go, uncondemned. Only after that does he say, 'Sin no more'. It is easy either to be judgmental or to have no standards. Jesus holds standards and mercy together and gets them in the right order. 'Neither do I condemn you; go, and sin no more': it must be one of the greatest lines in scripture.

I have the impression that many Christians are finding sin, guilt, confession, repentance and forgiveness harder to handle than was once the case. The matter abounds in paradoxes. One is that I notice this condemnatory phenomenon in the evangelical tradition to which I belong, despite the fact that it has always especially stressed the fact of forgiveness purely on the basis of what Jesus has done for us. Yet this same tradition has also been inclined to a form of legalism, a focus on lists of 'do's and 'don't's. Recently this has been less so, and we do not feel bound by the taboos of our spiritual forebears (e.g. over Sunday observance or alcohol). But we do not seem to be more free, more graceful. Many of us carry round a deep sense of being unworthy, of being stained, of not loving God enough, of not praying enough. It seems that we assume that Job's friends are right; our relationship with God depends on what we do, and if we do not do enough, then that relationship is imperilled. Our picture of God is of someone who always has a big stick hidden behind his back, ready to hit us. We often characterize the Pharisees in the Gospels as assuming that they could reach God by doing good; the fact that neither the Gospels nor other sources indicate that this was true of the Pharisees suggests that we may be the perpetrators and victims of the Freudian device of projection, whereby we attribute to other people the characteristics we cannot face in ourselves.

All those awarenesses of guilt are compounded by the more general sense of guilt among liberal and Christian people concerning the way we are spoiling the earth and oppressing the third world and living off the oppression of the past (e.g. of native Americans or native Australians). And all those awarenesses are destructive because we can do nothing about them except apparently trivial gestures such as signing petitions. So we just have to live with the guilt in the sense of living with the fact that we cannot avoid continuing to live in the wrong way.

The Harrison Ford courtroom drama *Presumed Innocent* was repeated on our television last night. It is a story of adultery, murder, guilt and punishment. Like a good suspense story it turns the plot upside-down during the last ten minutes, but then it actually ends with a soliloquy about punishment – not the punishment that the court imposes (for it does not) but the punishment imposed by the guilt with which the protagonists will live for the rest of their lives, knowing what they have done. It is a very moral film, but a very bleak one.

(ii)

Not many of us carry about the burden of guilt and punishment that the characters in *Presumed Innocent* do, but we have our guilts – not just guilt feelings but true guilts for what we have failed to do. For us Psalm 130 provides a way to pray and a model of repentant prayer.

Repentance involves recognizing the depth of our problem with sin. 'Out of the depths I cry to you O Lord' (verse 1). Praying out of the depths is a common idea in the Psalms. We pray overwhelmed by trouble, overburdened by pressures, pressed down by opposition; everything is on top of us. Here in Psalm 130 the problem is not our circumstances or fears or sufferings or doubts but our sins: not what life or other people or God have done to us, but what we have done with life and to other people and to God.

Both of those are important. I can see myself as someone needy, insecure, troubled and hurt, and come to God as the one who heals me. I can also see myself as responsible, self-centred, failed and guilty, and come to God as the one who forgives me. In the churches I know best, it used to be the case that the second of those was emphasized and the first ignored. The problem is now the opposite: healing has all the focus.

So Psalm 130 puts an important challenge before us. It asks us whether we see ourselves as sinners, as in very deep water because of our sin. The psalm implies that we need to be specific about it. It speaks not just of sin but of sins such as God might keep a detailed record of (verse 3). If we do not see where our areas of sin are, we may need to do some enquiring of God (and some enquiring of other people!).

Repentance involves bowing before the graciousness of a forgiving God (verse 4). Once we do see that we are in deep water because of sin, that can be deeply discouraging. It can suggest we have a rather *1984*-kind of God, one who indeed carries a stick behind his back ready to punish us. 'Every step you take, every smile you fake, I'll be watching you.' 'If you, O Lord, kept a record of sins, O Lord, who could stand?'

The words remind us of the tax-collector who could not stand before God because he felt he would be shrivelled by God's justice, or of Peter shrinking back from Jesus with his 'depart from me because I am a sinful man, Lord,' or of another psalm with its awed contemplation of the fact that wherever we go God is able to reach us – we can never get away (see Psalm 139).

But in God's eyes it is not like that. The last word of verse 2 has already hinted at it. The word is 'grace' (the NIV translates it 'mercy'). It is the kind of grace we are familiar with in human experience when someone else has every reason to be extremely angry with us and we are amazed to find that they are not. That is how God is. Forgiveness is 'with' God (verse 4): it is God's next-door-neighbour, God's nearest and dearest. It is the very essence of God.

It would be easy to take that for granted and trade on it. Instead, the psalm says, that is why God is feared, held in awe (verse 4). Suppose you have let someone down and they do not hold it against you. If you are really sorry, you do not then trade on that; you try to do what is best and least hassle for them. So it is between us and God. Grace and forgiveness are of the essence of God; and they make us bow before God.

Repentance involves trusting in the word of God (verse 5). In human relationships, we may not know whether we will be forgiven. Nervously we confess that we have made some mistake, not knowing what the reaction will be. We wait anxiously for the response of the person we have wronged.

So the psalm likens our anxiety to someone watching and waiting for the morning (verse 6). Perhaps it refers to the ministers in the temple watching for the dawn and the moment when they are due to offer the morning sacrifice, perhaps to sentries keeping watch in case an enemy attacks – so that dawn means another night is safely over. Either way it is a keen-eyed anticipation.

With that keenness we wait for the word of God. Will God forgive? It is his job, Voltaire said. No, says the psalm, you cannot take it for granted. After all, there was more than one occasion in the scriptures when a prayer for forgiveness was refused because God knew that people were not really repentant and had not really changed (see, for example, Jeremiah 14:7–10).

But in another sense we can be sure that if we really do turn back to God, God will forgive. Jonah knew that – it was the reason why he did not want to go and preach to the Ninevites. The God of Israel is compassionate, gracious and long-suffering (Exodus 34:6–7). Forgiveness is indeed this God's business.

Repentance involves receiving something which it is then our privilege to share (verse 7). The psalm pictures God giving us both forgiveness and freedom, both mercy and redemption (verses 7–8). Real repentance cannot mean that I stay as I was before. God frees me from sin's penalty and thereby also frees me from sin's power. My problem is that I am in bondage to guilt and self-centredness, and repentance and forgiveness free me from both of these.

That is the psalm's testimony. It speaks of the freedom that comes from being forgiven. The psalm is indeed a testimony at this point. It speaks to other people, not directly to God. It presupposes that everything that God does for me is done not just for me but for other people. We tell each other what God has done for us individually, and that builds up faith and worship and leads to God getting the glory. We weep with those who weep, and we rejoice with those who rejoice.

After watching *Presumed Innocent* again, I went to bed awed and grateful that in the real world the Jesus who died and rose is one who makes it both necessary and possible to face guilt and then to live with it in a way that prevents its being a weight hanging round one's neck for ever. That is something to tell the world and the church about.

(iii)

So what God does for us is also done for a non-Christian world that knows that it is guilty and in bondage to the past, and to other people, and to the world, and to oneself. A best-selling album by Prefab Sprout includes a simple song which opens 'Mercy on me, O say that I'm forgiven and wrap your arms around me' and adds 'To your goodness I surrender. Without mercy where is goodness?'

Yes, that is the world's need, but it is also the need of a church full of people whose sense of guilt spoils their lives and who need a sense of forgiveness to remake them. Perhaps it is significant that the composer of the song, Paddy McAloon, was once an ordinand.

The composer Gavin Bryars tells how he acquired some unused film of people living rough in London, including footage of a tramp singing

> Jesus' blood never failed me yet.
> There's one thing I know, for he loves me so.

Bryars was moved by it and wanted to do something with it, looping the tape and adding accompaniment so as eventually to produce an album and then an even longer CD version with the quirky American singer Tom Waits. 'When I copied the loop onto the continuous reel in Leicester,' at the Polytechnic, where he worked, Bryars says, 'I left the door of the recording studio open while I went downstairs to get a cup of coffee. When I came back I found the normally lively room unnaturally subdued. People were moving about much more slowly than usual, and a few were sitting alone, quietly weeping.'

In contrast, Lou Reed and John Cale, two members of the Velvet Underground, might seem markedly anti-religious characters. *Songs For Drella* was their tribute to Andy Warhol after he died, their way of coming to terms with grief and guilt.

In the last track Lou Reed talks to Warhol as if he were still alive, about wishing he had talked with him more before his death, about how he had misinterpreted the artist's shyness, about how he misses talking with him and watching him paint. He remembers turning away from Warhol the last time he saw him because of things that had got between them, and sings about 'resentments that can never be unmade', and about the fact that making an album is the only way a musician knows to try to express regret. It closes: 'Hello, it's me – goodnight, Andy. Goodbye, Andy'.

16

Retro-reading

(i)

There is a hymn by Brian Wren called 'Sing my song backwards'. The idea of it is that there is a sense in which you always have to understand the gospel story from where it ends. When you hear the account of Jesus being crucified, or undertaking his ministry, or being baptized, or being born, you know that this is a story that ends with him being raised in glory, and that makes a difference to the way you read the story as a whole. That is one level on which the Gospels themselves work, in different ways. Their accounts of Jesus' life and death are the story of someone who is on the way to being raised in glory.

So Luke's Gospel, for instance, starts with an explanation of why Luke is telling his story. It is because it is the basis of Christian faith; these are the things that have been fulfilled, and witnessed to, and preached. The opening of Luke's Gospel presupposes that Jesus is risen and that there is a gospel. When he has explained that, Luke goes back to the beginning of the Jesus story, and we read it in the light of where it is going. Even when we read the opening account of something that happened fifteen months before Jesus was born, we read about this event in the light of the resurrection of Jesus.

Luke is inviting us to live together through this story from the lives of Elizabeth and Zechariah. Imagine yourself as one of these two people.

You live in the time of Herod, the Herod who built the temple, and who might seem to be someone on your side. But he has built shrines to other gods as well, and fortresses such as Caesarea and Sebastia and the Antonia in Jerusalem, all in honour of Roman rulers, Roman oppressors. It was they who made him king; he is a foreigner and had no right to the throne. He is someone who always has reason to feel insecure about his position, and someone who has no hesitation about slaughtering anyone who looks like a threat to him – the Hasmonean family, who had a claim to his throne because they were the successors of the Maccabees, or the baby boys of Bethlehem because one of them was supposed to be on the way to the throne of his ancestor David.

You are a man or a woman who lives under that kind of political regime. Imagine living under whatever oppressive regime is making the headlines as you read this; or imagine living in Jerusalem itself today. Imagine the insecurity, the subjection, the constraint, the shame, the disgust, the longing for a better future.

You live in the time of King Herod. You belong to the tribe of Aaron, the tribe of priests. It is a position to be proud of. But you have not let that go to your head. You are someone who puts God first, someone who lives the whole of life before God and walks in God's way. You are someone distinguished for your position, but also distinguished for your personal piety.

But you are also someone with a personal inner grief. You have not been able to have children. You tried for years, saw doctors and hoped and prayed, but it never happened. Now you are in your forties and it looks as if it never will happen.

Yet you know the stories about Sarah and Abraham, and Manoah and his wife, and Hannah and Elkanah. Sometimes you have shared those stories with other people in distress like yours, and you have told people that this God is our God, and that has sharpened the hurt that it does not seem to apply to you. You know that pain keeps the heart soft, and of course you know that the God of Israel is a great God and that the privilege of serving that God is worth everything, that having that God means you can live with any other pain.

But on the dark days, when people say how privileged you are to belong to the priestly tribe, the tribe of Aaron, inside you are tempted to say, 'I'd swap with anybody, I'd swap with a

164   *To The Usual Suspects*

Samaritan, if we could only have a baby.' And when you think about the way you seek to live close to God and walk in God's way, on the dark days you wonder whether it is worthwhile at all, and you ask what is the point, and wonder whether God is really there.

You are Zechariah or Elizabeth, with that experience. Outside of this fantasy you are also you. You are a person with a position to be proud of, a daughter or son of God. You are someone with a relationship with God to be proud of, someone who puts God first. Are you someone with a pain that casts a gloomy cloud over all that, on the dark days? Can you name your position and your commitment and your pain to the God of Elizabeth and Zechariah?

What kind of day is it today, Zechariah, Elizabeth? Workwise, it is a very special day. The priests were divided into worship teams, which served a week on and then had twenty-three weeks off, which is better than most churches rosters. If you were a priest and it was your week on, there were so many of you that they had to draw lots for the best privilege, for the task of being the priest who burnt the incense before the Lord in the temple. It was this person who actually sent the prayers of the people up to God. They crowded round the temple praying. You made the smoke go up, and you prayed for them, for God's blessing and peace, grace and compassion, to come to them from God. And then you came out and blessed them with that prayer that Moses gave the priests: 'The Lord bless you and keep you, the Lord smile on you and be gracious to you, and the Lord give you peace.' It was something you got the chance to do once in your life, if you were lucky.

And this is your day, Zechariah. And your day, Elizabeth, because it means a lot for you as well. Maybe you have asked yourself why women cannot take part in the way the men do. But all the same it is very precious to you that Zechariah can. In spirit you are with him there in the temple. And both of you are concentrating on Israel and God and the relationship between them, and Israel's need of God's grace, and their need for God to deliver them from their oppression. At least, you are trying to concentrate on that, because you know that this is a day more than any other for forgetting yourselves and your personal needs. But this is the most precious day of your ministry as a couple, the moment when your ministry takes you nearest to God, and you cannot help also being more aware than ever of the pain in your heart, and more agonized than ever by that puzzle at the centre of your relationship with God.

Then something happens to you, Zechariah. It is going to be a long time before he can tell you all about it, Elizabeth, but eventually you will hear it from his lips, and you can imagine every detail of the scene. There is somebody else there in the holy place, where there should only be Zechariah. A figure in white stands by the altar. It looks like another priest, and for a moment you thought it was, but there should not be anybody else there; and though the figure looks human, there is something about it that tells you it is not. You were keyed up already and a bit awestruck today, but now you are overcome by a different kind of awe.

The messenger knows that, and tells you not to be afraid. God has heard your prayer. But you have not really got through the prayers yet. What does the message mean? It means the prayer that arises from your own pain, the prayer you have often stopped praying, the pain you have stopped talking about to each other. God has heard that prayer. You, Elizabeth, are going to have a baby. But it does not just mean the prayer for a baby. It means the prayer for Israel as well. This baby is going to be the means of bringing Israel back to God, the means of preparing a people for the Lord. He will be God's answer to your personal prayer, and also God's answer to the prayer that arises out of your ministry. Your need and Israel's need, your prayer for yourselves and your prayer for God's purpose to be fulfilled, the two will be one when they are answered. It was all right to interweave your prayers for yourself and your prayers for your people, because God is inclined to interweave the answers.

This turns out to be an Easter-kind of story. It is a story about people with a deep pain in their hearts because God seems to have let them down – about people with a cross in their hearts. It is a story about an angel appearing and banishing fear and declaring that what seemed impossible and undreamable was about to become fact. It is a story about the reality of new life when there seemed only lifelessness and barrenness. It is a story about people whose personal pain was mixed up with the pain that their ministry had brought them, and about both these pains being healed by an act of God they hardly dared hope for.

Be yourself again for a moment. Name again that pain that lies hidden in you. Bring to mind the deep longing that you hardly dare make a matter of prayer because it is evidently not God's will to do anything about it, and thinking about it makes it worse. It is a deep longing which it is therefore best just to forget, and you do that, except for those moments in the night when you cannot and you cry out in the dark that this is your longing and it cannot be fulfilled. Imagine that you are standing before God praying for your people but aware of that pain of your own and that God says, 'Your prayer has been heard.' Imagine the impossibility becoming possibility.

I hesitated to invite you to do that because of the hurt that is involved. Merely on the basis of the story of Elizabeth and Zechariah I might not. But I can do it on the basis of reading the story backwards, beginning Luke's Gospel after Easter. The resurrection promises that the hope that came to Elizabeth and Zechariah is not the exception, it is the rule. I do not know how or when, but I know that there will be a fulfilment of that vision in Isaiah 25 of the veil of pain and grief and mourning that lies over us all being cast away when the Lord swallows up death in all its forms for ever and wipes away the tears from every face. It is Easter truth. It was too overwhelming a promise for Zechariah himself to cope with. But we have reason to believe it.

At the end of the story both of you, son and daughter of Aaron, have to go back home and get on with the job of life. You are a bit like the disciples after the resurrection. They are not due to go out to tell the world yet. You are not saying anything to anyone yet, Elizabeth. You go back to the same place, to the same tasks. But you go with a different hope, and with new life budding in the womb. You go singing a song that begins with the resurrection and only goes through crosses afterwards.

(ii)

It is daybreak in Jerusalem. Women are arriving from the villages around, with their bundles of herbs, eggs, and produce to sell near the city gate. They still come nowadays, dignified women, inscrutable. Behind their reserved faces you wonder what is going on inside their heads and their hearts. (They are victims of political intransigence on the part of Palestinian and Israeli men, but that is another story.)

There are also three women leaving Jerusalem. They, too, are women of reserve, dignity and inner pain, grieving for a man they all loved, a dead messiah. They are going to anoint his body. They are still coming to terms with the idea of his being dead, and perhaps they want to go and look at his body, to tell it that they cared. They are confused, and half-way there they realize they will not be able to get into the tomb because of the boulder in front of it.

It is not Easter Sunday in their lives yet. Spring, when the days get lighter and the trees bud, is a peak time for committing suicide. What the calendar says and what nature says conflicts with what is happening inside people; they cannot bear the difference. There was a South American Indian tribe exploited and oppressed by government, business and industry. At Easter they observed only Holy Week, not Easter Day. It was not real for them. We are not expected to jolly such people out of that, though we may look for the way God may want to bring Easter reality to them.

One Good Friday a Christian woman came to see me because she was being assaulted by her husband. She was trying to make the marriage work in a civilized way and to bring their children up happily, but he would turn on her, although she felt she was trying so hard. 'And there's no justice,' I remember her saying, with a Good Friday anguish. It had not changed much by Easter Day. It can still be Good Friday for us when the calendar says Easter Day. At least we can be with people on their Good Fridays.

Then the two Marys and Salome discover something which suggests that Good Friday has passed. The boulder has moved. Inside the tomb is a young man in a white suit looking as pleased as Punch, brushing specks of rock dust from his sleeves: 'How about that then?' ('All right, what do you do for an encore?') He has pushed the stone away, not to let Jesus out, for Jesus left a while ago, but to let people in to see that he has gone, to let witnesses see that the tomb is empty.

'No one's stolen the body,' the lad says. 'That's where he lay down, but he's got up, gone back to Galilee. He'll see you there. Bye.' And (whoosh) the young man is gone.

Jesus and his friends were never really at home in Jerusalem. Jesus had work to do there, but now he has done it, and he is back up north. Galilee was not quieter; it was busier in its way, more multi-ethnic, than Jerusalem. It was not safer; people had tried to kill Jesus there. Jerusalem just happened to be the place where they succeeded. It was not merely that Galilee was home; home was where they had first rejected him. Urban, multi-ethnic, un-fashionable, needy, hard Galilee was where God had first sent Jesus to preach and work signs of God's reign. So that is where he is off to. He will see them there, if they want to join him in his mission to that ordinary world.

Jesus had gone elsewhere just when he seemed bound to stay in one place. He is so unpredictable, always missing from where you thought you could find him, and present somewhere different from where you thought you had a right to expect. He promises to be somewhere, and when you get there you find that he was there but has now moved on again.

The women were prepared to face up to the fact that Jesus had become a corpse. They were not hiding from reality like the men. They were prepared to adjust, to begin living in the light of reality and loss, of pain and disappointment. Then they find that he is not there, the young man in the white suit says he is alive, and they are invited to go and tell the men, and Peter, and to begin hoping again.

'Tell the disciples and Peter.' Does Peter still count as a disciple, the man who first fell asleep, then disowned Jesus, then kept well away from the cross? People who have done things that make them wonder whether they still count as disciples are invited to put their own name in the sentence – 'Tell the disciples and . . . John (or whoever it is) that I will see them in Galilee.'

'So the women were thrilled to bits and ran to tell them.' Not on your life. At the beginning of the story they are grieving and hurt, at the end trembling and bewildered, running scared and not telling anyone anything. After all, imagine your business is about to fold. You are just getting used to the idea when someone says there is a miracle solution. Do you believe them, just like that, and rush out to tell the world? Aren't you afraid, half-wishing they had not told you because you don't know where you are again now, you don't know what to believe? 'It's not the despair I can't stand, it's the hope.'

The women's silence cannot be the end of what happened, otherwise we would not know about it. Indeed, this is a wholly strange account of Jesus' resurrection. Jesus is not even there. Perhaps that enables us to put ourselves into the story. We live our lives between an empty tomb and a Jesus who is already over the horizon, only a cloud of dust. We do not see Jesus being raised from the dead. We have the evidence. There is no corpse in the tomb. He is gone. But it happened before we got here. We did not see him.

Nor can we see Jesus with us now. We will see him when he appears at the End, but that is in the future. We may miss what he is doing or saying in the present because we are blind to it, like those disciples. Mark says to us, 'Open your eyes, get your walking boots on, Jesus is alive, he is off to work in the world, if you hurry you can catch up with him and join in. The Twelve are disillusioned and demoralized, they may not be there. Even the women are beside themselves with fear. Nobody will do it unless you and I do.'

17

Struggle

'How vast are the resources of God's power open to us as believers. His mighty strength was seen at work when he raised Christ from the dead.' So the beginning of Ephesians (1:19, 20a). It is part of its resurrection gospel. Jesus' being raised to a transformed life is not merely a fact about him (though it is that). It also shows potentials available to us.

At the end of the letter that theme comes back. It is not so obvious that this is also an Easter passage, but it is. 'Finally, find your strength in the Lord, in his mighty power' (6:10). The strength we are told is available to us is the power that brought Jesus from the dead. As Bishop David Jenkins once said, that is not just the power to resuscitate a bag of bones, which medics will be able to do one day. It is the power to give Jesus a new kind of life, the life of the new age and the new heavens and the new earth. That power is available to us.

And it needs to be. Because 'our struggle is not against human foes, but against cosmic powers, against the authorities and potentates of this dark age, against the superhuman forces of evil in the heavenly realms. That is why you must take up the armour of God' (6:12–13a).

There was a moment in our fellowship group at college one year when we were praying for each other, and I found myself thinking round the group and realizing that in virtually every one of these people God had been at work in different ways. I knew how God had been at work, and I knew that it was often in painful ways. In each case spiritual progress was being made, but somehow it tended to be hard work. Indeed, I saw that what was true of these individuals was true of college as a whole. The picture that came into my mind was of trench warfare. The image meshed with pictures that one or two people in the group had had on other occasions that term. We were an army who had been making progress that year. But every inch had had to be fought for, every yard had been hard work, every foot paid for in blood, every centimetre required huge effort because it met resistance. We had been advancing, but it had been like trench warfare.

Indeed, other things had happened which could have made us doubt whether God was really at work. As happens in communities, there were things that had threatened to waste unnecessary energy, things that led people to misunderstand each other. And those are the marks of our being in a battle, with forces that like to discourage and deceive. It is a battle in which we are on the way to the blessing that God promises to us, but progress towards that blessing involves struggle. It is not a blessing that is easily reached, as we might presuppose at some springlike moments of our life with God. It is a blessing reached only through conflict. Because 'our struggle is not against human foes, but against cosmic powers, against the authorities and potentates of this dark age' (6:12–13a).

The Bible does not go into great detail about the nature of the spiritual forces we contend with. It does not seem to know more than you and I know, that there is more to evil than meets the eye. It is not just the sum of its parts. The way we experience it makes that clear. The Bible assumes that and does not tell you much more about it, but concentrates on pointing you to the way of victory.

We are involved in a struggle against the ruling forces that are masters in a dark age. The powers of evil specialize in ruling, in exercising authority. As far as one can see from Genesis, there was no authority structure designed for human life in the world except the one contained in God. There was no authority of one human being over another until after sin came into the world: that was when people began to exercise domination over each other. There was no headship, no government. Human authority and resistance to human authority both belong to this age, not to the age of creation or the age of new creation. Whenever human authority is being exercised, we are in the realm where the powers of darkness operate.

That applies to the world and to the church. When rectors or archdeacons or bishops give in to the temptation to act in an authoritarian way, or in a manipulative way, they act under the influence of the powers of darkness. When church councils or clergy either accept that kind of authority or rebel against it (you should listen to clergy talking about their bishops), they are working with the assumption that the church operates as an institution that belongs by its inner nature to this age. They are colluding with the powers of darkness. The same is true in a Christian community such as a theological college, in the way principal, tutors, and students operate. We get sucked into a way of working that is the way of the powers of darkness.

Ephesians tells us what are our weapons and our protection in this conflict.

> Stand fast. Fasten on the belt of truth; for a breastplate put on integrity; let the shoes on your feet be the gospel of peace; and with all these take up the great shield of faith, with which you will be able to quench all the burning arrows of the evil one. Accept salvation as your helmet, and the sword which the Spirit gives you, the word of God. (6:14–17)

There are two types of thing that this armour and weaponry stand for. There are things that involve us in doing something, and things we simply receive. The experts vary on the way they decide which are which, but both are there. The straightforward way to read the passage, I think, is to reckon that it talks first about three things that involve us doing something: truth, integrity, and witness. Then it talks about three things that are more matters of what we receive: faith, salvation, and the gospel.

The three things that involve our activity all come from Isaiah (see 11:5; 59:17; 52:7). Truth is the belt that holds you together. Not *the* truth, which would mean the gospel, but simply truth.

It is a phrase that describes the armour the messiah wears. Our own uprightness is one of the things that holds us together in battle. And integrity as our breastplate protects us back and front. It is a phrase that describes the armour God wears in battle, in Isaiah. Our own straightness protects us. The third item of equipment is the gospel of peace on our feet: the phrase takes up that quaint talk in Isaiah about beautiful feet bringing good news of peace to the exiles. Our activity involves our being people of truth, integrity and encouragement.

When I had had that picture of trench warfare I went to talk with one of my colleagues about how it might apply to college, and we talked about various things, which later I found with some others in Ephesians 6 – typically the Bible had got there first. My colleague's word for those aspects of the soldier's armour which point to our responsibility was the word 'holiness'. 'What do you mean?' I asked him. He hesitated for a split second, and then said; 'Sexual purity. I don't mean I suspect that there are things going on that shouldn't be,' he said. 'It's just that I know from my own heart that that is an area we always have to protect.' If we are in a battle, this is an area that we are bound to need to protect, or one where we are bound to need protection.

It is not merely a question of sex outside marriage being wrong, partly because we who are married can then be let off too lightly. Selfish sex within marriage is also sinful. I wonder whether one of the key questions anybody has to ask about any relationship is how far it is actually selfish, how far I am in it for the other person's benefit. That is surely one of the key moral questions about sexual relations. To put it crudely, it is not merely a question of what you do with certain bits of your body. It is about how fair what you are doing is, it is about why you are doing it, it is about what in the end this activity and this relationship will do to this other person, and to other people to whom you and they have commitments. Those questions are raised sharply and perhaps unanswerably by every act of extra-marital sex, but they are also raised uncomfortably by every act of marital sex. Is it really an act of love? It is interesting that God's words to Eve in Genesis 3 put together authoritarianism and sexual selfishness as the consequences of humanity's disobedience: 'Your desire will be for your husband and he will rule over you.' To love and to cherish becomes to desire and to dominate (Derek Kidner in his commentary on Genesis).

Sexual relationships have become for our age a key means by which you realize yourself, and Christians are inevitably affected by that sort of expectation. It is interesting that in the preceding chapter of Ephesians the question of the significance of sex has been raised in quite different terms. There we get explicit instruction on the significance of sex, with the only explicit biblical teaching on the headship of a man over his wife. It makes it absolutely clear that there is a biblical doctrine of headship, and it makes it clear what that doctrine is. It is that men have the unquestionable right and responsibility to let themselves be crucified for women, and that women must submit to them in the sense of letting them do that.

Typical that scripture should take a worldly assumption and let the cross turn it upside-down. The world says – or did in that culture – 'men have authority over women.' The Bible says, 'Yes, they have the authority Christ showed on the cross.' Biblical headship is nothing at all to do with men deciding how to bring up the children or where the family should live. It is about letting yourself be walked on. That is the Bible's pattern for relations between the sexes. Marriage gives you lots of chances to live that way; single people are called to make that their criterion for their relationships too. In our relationships the other person comes first. My hunch is that although there may sometimes seem to be little chance of marital relations being that way, there is even less chance with extramarital ones – they are even more likely to end up in hurt rather than in love.

Truth, integrity and encouragement are responsibilities we exercise, important ones if we are to be protected in our conflict. Let them be the way we relate to one another as sexual beings. There will be other areas of holiness we have to think about, of course, and we will also need to think out what truth and integrity and encouragement mean there.

Then there are the shield, which is faith, and the helmet, which is salvation, and the Spirit's sword, which is the word God speaks.

They all sound more like things you receive. So here in Ephesians the challenge comes first, and the grace you need to meet the challenge comes second. We certainly need the gospel at this point, because we all fail as sexual beings, just as we fail in the way we cope with exercising authority or reacting to it, and in other areas. We can be driven into more failure precisely by the awareness of failure and guilt. We need armour to protect us from that.

It is not just the feeling of guilt, which again as people of our particular era we may be inclined to concentrate on, but the fact of guilt. We carry that around with us: the things that we know we have done, the things we wish we had done, the fantasies we would like to turn into realities. They become unbearable burdens that drive us into more failure, unless the gospel gets applied to them. So Ephesians challenges us about our responsibilities and then reassures us about our resources. Faith quenches all the fiery darts of the evil one. The evil one throws our failures into our face, loves to make us feel more and more guilty and paralysed and driven to despair and to more failure. Faith showers our face clean and quenches those burning arrows.

How does 'faith' do that? Not because it is a matter of faith in faith, but because it is a matter of faith in Christ as our saviour. There is not a lot of difference between many of these pieces of armour. They are using poetic imagery, not offering an excerpt from a martial arts catalogue. To talk about the shield of faith is really the same as to talk about the helmet of salvation. The sword which the Holy Spirit gives us to wield at the evil one is the gospel.

Suppose the evil one rubs my nose in the fact that I am a sexual failure – not in the sense that the world thinks of sexual failure; in those terms I might be a sexual success. But in terms of my relationships being something through which I express integrity, uprightness and encouragement I might be a failure. That is then the point at which Jesus utters those wonderful words in John's Gospel: 'I do not condemn you.' Those are the kind of gospel words about salvation which my faith clings to and which I throw back in the evil one's face with a grin when I am reminded that I have been a failure. The word of God is the Spirit's sword. And when I've done that, I can also face the words Jesus goes on to utter: 'Neither do I condemn you. You can go. Sin no more.' The armour includes the shield of faith, the helmet of salvation, and the Spirit's sword, the word of the gospel. If we are to make progress in this trench warfare with the evil one who will do anything to prevent us getting to the place of blessing which God's promise has set before us, we had better keep that armour on.

There is one more thing this paragraph of Ephesians presses on us. 'Constantly ask God's help in prayer, and pray always in the power of the Spirit. To this end keep watch and persevere, always interceding for all God's people. Pray also for me' (6:18–19a). Prayer is a subject on which it is even easier than is the case with sex to make people feel guilty rather than free. These words in Ephesians are an exhortation: they are about the responsibility of prayer, but they are not designed to make us feel guilty but to remind us of another resource we have in the spiritual battle we wage together. Feel encouraged, if you like, that the New Testament has to keep reminding you to pray and that the Old Testament includes so many examples of how to pray – they indicate that people did not find it easy then, so we need not feel inferior.

'Pray at all times with all prayer and supplication.' 'Keep alert with all perseverance, making supplication for all the saints,' the RSV puts it more literally. In his commentary on Ephesians, John Stott points out that it does not say 'sometimes with some prayer and some perseverance for some of your brothers and sisters', but all prayer and all perseverance for all the saints at all times. Perhaps Christians might think about covenanting to pray for each other in that way as they engage in their trench warfare with the evil one. It sounds like another key to the battle for the blessing being won. Perhaps it would be the blessing.

'Keep watch,' we are told. 'Be alert' – the church needs lerts (the old jokes are the best jokes). Be alert. Take Jesus on Maundy Thursday as your model for the way you operate by resurrection power from Easter Tuesday. The power that brought Jesus from the dead is available to us, and it needs to be if we are to reach the blessing God has promised us. It is not just the power to resuscitate a bag of bones, it is the power to give Jesus a wholly new kind of life, the life of the new age and the new heavens and the new earth. It is available to us.

18

Tears

I cannot remember whether I used to cry ten years ago. I do not think I was especially averse to crying or was embarrassed by the idea or felt that I had to keep a stiff upper lip in all circumstances. I do not remember it being an issue. But I am aware that in recent years I have found myself crying relatively often.

Like many people (women, anyway), I cry in films. I wept near the end of *Once Upon a Time in America* and *Paris, Texas* and *When Harry Met Sally* and *The English Patient* and *Leaving Las Vegas*, I remember. I am sure there are others, but those are among my favourite films. I howled on our sofa at the end of reading *The Bridges of Madison County*, before seeing the film. I wept at the beginning of *Sleepless in Seattle* and again at the end: it was the only time I wept at both ends of a film, I think, but there was reason in terms of the story. In all those films there is something about the toughness of human experience, about pain or loss, about guilt or helplessness, about bondage to our personalities or our past, about bravery or acceptance of the inevitable, or occasionally about happiness which you did not believe would ever come (even if at head-level you knew the plot required it).

Unlike many people, perhaps (or perhaps not!), I sometimes want to cry in my own sermons, and essentially for the same sort of reasons. I used to preach a sermon on Samson (before it appeared in print in *After Eating the Apricot*) and I always had to hold back a tear at the last line of it, at the fact that Samson who fell so far short of all he should have been is in the cloud of witnesses in Hebrews 11: 'and if there is room for Samson, there is room for you and me'. And in this book I have referred to a number of occasions when I have found myself in tears. Looking back over the chapters, I discover that I have wept because at one level I was afraid lest I could not sustain the demands that my job placed on me. I have wept at the reminder of the commitment I made to let God be my only desire. I have wept in talking students through the story of Job. I have wept through becoming overwhelmingly aware of God's love. I have wept in saying goodbye to people, at losing people. I have wept in recognizing my loneliness and the length of the journey and the number of rivers there are to cross. I have wept in having to take Ann for a routine stay at her rehabilitation centre. I have wept at the awareness of God's rejoicing in me. I have thus wept at sad moments, and more strikingly at moments of joy. I have found how weeping our own tears and discovering what they mean may be part of acknowledging hurts and sins from which we have hidden and may thus be part of finding forgiveness and healing.

So tears are strange things. Maggie Ross has written a book about tears called *The Fountain and the Furnace: The Way of Tears and of Fire* (Paulist, 1987). She talks about the connection between the gift of tears and the gift of joy, and about the way tears unlock joy. They can signify that we are giving up self, and thus finding self; so in death is life. The salt of tears is the savour of life (pp. 21, 22, 29). Tears, she says, are a mark of having touched reality (p. 227). I have mentioned John of the Cross, who talks much (as other mystical writers do) of our love relationship with Jesus. He often refers to scripture in this connection, especially to the Song of Songs. The trouble is that the Song of Songs seems originally to have been a collection of ordinary human love songs, not poems about our love for God. That awareness about the original meaning of John's favourite book sent me off on a hunt for passages of scripture which directly refer to an emotional love relationship between us and God. These turned out to be hard to find. I was then interested to discover that the person who most clearly reveals an emotional love for Jesus does so with tears (Luke 7:38).

I can think of four possible reasons for my own greater susceptibility to tears. The first is that I have grown older. One of the things that happens, they say, as you come to middle age is that sides of your personality that you had not previously realized can find expression – you can own your 'shadow side'. For me, tears may be part of the complement to a hardness with both positive and negative sides which was more characteristic of me for my first forty-odd years. The second is that because of Ann's illness I have felt more pain over the past ten years than in earlier years of my life. The third is related to those first two. It is that the tears issue from having God pierce a way into my life through the fact that Ann and I have had to live with Ann's illness. That has perhaps reached into me and brought to the surface realities and capacities that would otherwise have lain unrealized.

The fourth is quite unrelated, except in the providence of God (which is quite an exception). The tears link in some way to being a theological college principal (others who have occupied this position will allow themselves a wry smile, or a wry tear). I felt some ambiguity about becoming a principal. I used to say that I had no desire or need to be in charge of the college, to be the number one, to carry that responsibility. I deserve to have had someone say (perhaps they did say behind my back) (no, they were the kind of people who said things to one's face) that I behaved as if I was in charge of the place even when I was not, and in that sense I had no need to be formally in charge. I had the advantages of being involved in leadership without the disadvantage of formal responsibility. It was certainly the case that one of the great things about the college, which I remember discovering in my first staff meeting, was that if you had a good idea, it would be recognized and accepted even if you were the most junior person in the place. Conversely, if you could not get people to recognize the strength of your ideas, mere seniority in the system would not enable you to get them implemented.

On the other hand, I may secretly have suspected that as principal I would have the opportunity to exercise different forms of influence. I could shape agenda (literally and metaphorically) and set styles and throw my weight about. Once in a meeting when we were discussing a proposal I said very firmly something like 'I cannot agree to our doing that', and we decided not to do it. Later over tea there was an interesting discussion about (a) whether I was vetoing the proposal, and (b) whether people let it fall because they thought I was vetoing it, or (c) whether people let it fall because I felt so strongly about it. I did not know what I was doing, though if challenged I think I would have seen the remark as a contribution to debate not an end to debate, and I would have recognized (indeed in the discussion I pointed out) that I had no power to veto things. But subconsciously I may have intended the ambiguity and may have been intending to short-circuit debate.

Becoming principal meant that my relationship with power became more ambiguous than it had been previously. It was about then that I became acquainted with the writings of Maggie Ross. In her later book *Pillars of Flame: Power, Priesthood and Spiritual Maturity* (SCM, 1988: p. 38) she takes up the conviction that priesthood ought to reflect God and who God is in Christ.

> What God does is God's priesthood reaching across the abyss of illusion we create by presumption to control. As God's image we seek to mirror God's outpouring. God creates with self-abnegation outpoured, continues and sustains this creation *by going to the heart of pain that dwells within the Creator's self-restraint and is inherent in creation's freedom, and from this total self-denudation God generates new life, hope, and joy* (her emphasis).

So tears are central to emptying oneself of one's glory; they 'are a sign that we are struggling with power of one sort or another: the loss of ours; the entering of God's' (p. 124). More generally

> if we are to mirror God, to be in God's image . . . we have to be willing to enter our individual wounds and through them the wounds of the community. . . . We have to be willing to enter the wound of God. We have to be willing to enter these wounds, not hide them by casuistry, not seal them up, nor scar them over (p. xvii).

We can attempt to avoid this by seeking pseudo-healing which removes from us the possibility of the resurrection that comes through 'learning to live with, in, and through pain, to adjust to our wounding' (p.xviii).

In recent years there has been some talk of 'the gift of tears'. That talk invites us to see tears as inspired by the Spirit in a way which perhaps parallels tongues – each is both wordless and expressive. Tears are a gift which may make us able to empathize with others, to express our prayer for them in a physical way, to free them to express their own hurt or joy, and to free ourselves to express ours. What my own experience reflects is that if there is anything spiritual about tears, they have the same mixture of supernatural and natural as other gifts do (not least tongues).

Besides Isaac the Syrian, whom Maggie Ross refers to, one of the other classic writers on tears is Teresa of Avila. She was a sixteenth-century Spanish spiritual writer, like John of the Cross. In *The Interior Castle*, one of the great classics on the development of our relationship with God, she notes that tears can be of supernatural or of very natural significance.

> I have seen people shed tears over some great [natural] joy; sometimes, in fact, I have done it myself. It seems to me that the feelings which come to us from Divine things are as purely natural as these, except that their source is nobler. . . . Worldly joys have their source in our own nature and end in God, whereas spiritual consolations have their source in God, but we experience them in a natural way. . . .
>
> If I began to weep over the Passion, I could not stop until I had a splitting headache; and the same thing happened when I wept for my sins. This was a great grace granted to me by Our Lord, and I will not for a moment examine each of these two favours and decide which is the better. . . . The tears and longings sometimes arise partly from our nature and from the state of preparedness we are in; but nevertheless . . . they eventually lead one to God.
>
> Note also that distress of this kind is apt to be caused by weak health, especially in emotional people, who weep for the slightest thing; again and again they will think they are weeping for reasons which have to do with God but this will not be so in reality.

Do not let us suppose that if we weep a great deal we have done everything that matters. . . . Let the tears come when God is pleased to send them: we ourselves should make no efforts to induce them. They will leave this dry ground of ours well watered and will be of great help in producing fruit; but the less notice we take of them, the more they will do.

If we find ourselves in tears, it can be something which God sends or which God uses, or it can be something of purely human significance. Many people use up three tissues in a film, under cover of darkness. Any mother comes to allow for tears that are merely an attempt at manipulation, and God is not won over by the mere sight of tears (Malachi 2:13; Hebrews 12:17). They need to be an indication that something profound is going on or to be taken as a clue to something. They need to be an expression of true grief and not mere remorse, of true love and not of mere self-love.

In scripture and in Christian history, tears have been a natural part of praying for other people, and of praying for oneself. They vividly express the complex interweaving of body, spirit, feelings, mind, and subconscious. Sometimes we may be aware that all five are working together. Sometimes tears well up for reasons that mind may not yet know.

In the prayers in Psalms, people draw attention to their own tears. There could of course be a danger that these tears have become self-conscious and calculated, but in letting these prayers appear in scripture, God is apparently prepared to take that risk. In the prayers people use all sorts of devices in seeking to gain God's attention to their pain and hurt, and drawing attention to their tears is one such device. 'All night long I flood my bed with weeping and drench my couch with tears' (Psalm 6:6) or 'crying has been my food and drink' (Psalm 42:3) may seem exaggerations, but perhaps in the same way as 'I cried my eyes out' or 'I cried my heart out'. If we are hurt, the Psalms assume, the natural thing is to cry; and if we are hurt before God, we cry before God and expect God to notice, as a child cries before its mother and expects her to notice (cf. Psalm 39:12; 56:8). Crying turns out to be one of the things we need to learn from children.

I have referred to an occasion when I found myself weeping for a student who had a particular pain in his life. There was probably a selfish element to those tears. I saw my own loss mirrored in his. I was weeping for myself as well as for him. But I was weeping for him, and my feeling of grief meant I was putting myself in his place and weeping with one who was weeping. When that happens to us, we are involved in intercession. As the Bible sees it, intercession involves standing in someone else's place and speaking for them, speaking as them, identifying with them. If I weep for them, I can ask God to preserve these tears too, to note these tears, even as I may ask God to note mine, to preserve mine, to be motivated by mine. Jeremiah was once referred to as the 'weeping prophet', and that was what he himself wanted to be. He wanted to overflow unceasingly with tears for his own people because of the loss that their own sin had put them through and because this sin threatened to put them through more loss (see Jeremiah 9:1; 14:17). His tears accompany his pleading with God not to cast the people off, not to act as if despising them, not to keep afflicting them like the oppressors observed by Ecclesiastes who cause people to weep without self-consciousness or calculation because of their oppression (Ecclesiastes 4:1), not to abandon the covenant relationship with the people (14:19–21).

Jeremiah's tears also accompany his verbalizing on the people's behalf of the confession of sin which is needed if God is to heed that prayer (14:20). Those tears over their sin are shed in their stead (they are tears they should shed). Other tears at their sin are shed because of his own grief at that sin and his awareness of where it will lead (13:17). Paul similarly weeps over the enemies of the cross of Christ (Philippians 3:18). In a parallel way he weeps when he faces people with ultimate questions in his preaching (Acts 20:19, 31; 2 Corinthians 4:4). When Jesus wept over the city of Jerusalem, he takes up Jeremiah's ministry (Luke 19:41–44).

As we cannot have the joy of prayer answered without praying some prayers, so we cannot have the joy of tears wiped away without having shed some (cf. Luke 6:21). That applies both to tears on our own behalf and to tears we weep for others. But if we have shed some tears, then we can prove that those who sow in tears (not believing that there can ever be a harvest again, that the laughter of the past can ever be laughter in the present) do reap in joy (Psalm 126). And we can know that the sending of disaster that causes tears is not God's last word: see Isaiah 25:8, taken up in Revelation 7:17; 21:4.

Jesus' ministry shows that this wiping away of tears is not an experience for which we necessarily have to wait until the End. He acts on behalf of the weeping widow at Nain and therefore she can stop weeping (Luke 7:13). At Bethany he does not merely tell people they have no need to weep; he first allows himself to be drawn into their weeping (John 11:31–35). He asks Mary Magdalene why she is weeping and in addressing her by name wipes away her tears (John 20:11–16) (I mistyped that as 'weeps away her tears', which bears thinking about).

19

Trust

As I write I am in the midst of my first serious exercise in trust for thirty years. I feel as if I am walking a plank or a tightrope with deep water below.

Mark Knopfler's song 'Love Over Gold' was already in my all-time top three, but now I feel that it describes not only the person I might wish I was, but in a way the person I have been forced to be over the past few months, pushed onto a high wire by God.

The song is addressed to someone who walks out on the high wire and dances on thin ice without paying heed to the danger or to people's advice. She (I presume) goes dancing through doorways just to see what she will find, and embodies the need to value 'love over gold', throw caution to the wind and take the risk of sharing love with strangers. One should not be held back by the possibility that 'the things that you hold can fall and be shattered, or run through your fingers like dust'.

A year ago I had a phone call from the Dean of the School of Theology at Fuller Theological Seminary in Pasadena, near Los Angeles. We had met four years previously in South Africa and I knew a number of the faculty at Fuller, and we had talked about the possibility of my visiting there one day to teach a course or two. This can simply be an interesting thing to do in its own right, but it can also be a way of testing out whether they might like to offer a post to someone, and I knew that they had an Old Testament post to fill.

I had been principal of St John's College, Nottingham, for nearly nine years, and at that stage I think I began to solidify in the expectation that ten years would probably be enough. At St John's we were involved in a major development project, and that time frame seemed likely to see the back of the process broken, which would make that a feasible time for a change. In the New Year I was still feeling fixed enough to buy a new VCR and to join a book club, yet I began to feel more rather than less unsettled. It began to seem that there were ways in which it would be good to have a change of principal sooner rather than later. As the college was already developing in interesting ways, but facing some pressing challenges, I believed it needed a differently shaped person at the helm. And this meshed with my own feeling of tiredness with the responsibility of being principal, to which I have already referred. I had felt that tiredness before, but had sensed God saying that I must gird up my loins and promising to be my strength, but this time I felt that God was giving me permission to give up.

A few weeks afterwards I heard a sermon from a bishop on the importance of not giving up, and I might have expected to be thrown by that, but instead found myself reacting, 'Yes, that's true in principle, but I know that God is saying something different to me at this moment.'

One evening I expressed the unsettled-ness to a friend, and that helped hugely to make me feel settled about feeling unsettled and thus able to regain peace and joy in Christ. I began to solidify over the idea of visiting Fuller after Easter so that if they offered me a job and we liked it, I might agree to go, and thus resign my post at St John's. But over the next weekend I realized that I wanted to dissociate the two questions. Whether it was time to leave St John's and where else we should go were two separate questions. From the college's angle, if I resigned early in the year rather than leaving it till after Easter, it could get ahead with appointing my successor, with the prospect of a straight handover in the summer. From my angle, there simply were two separate questions, and once I had got clear on one, it seemed strange to make it depend on the other.

In the event, there was another advantage. St John's has been a lovely place for Ann. There have been many people there who have loved her, and our house and garden have been delights to her. If we had reached a point where I was asking the question, 'Shall we leave here where Ann is at home and go to the USA where she does not want to go?', it would have been hard to do the latter. Somehow handling the questions one by one made it easier.

The day I was writing to the college council and to the tutorial staff to tell them that I intended to resign, a student wrote to me to say the things about community which I quoted in Chapter 5. I told another of our friends, who said that for a while she too had been feeling led to pray for us, without knowing why. I told one of Ann's companions, who said that her husband had been sensing a special impetus to pray for us, without knowing why. I took these as signs that we had been surrounded by God's protection over the preceding weeks and that the decision to go was right (which another friend pointed out to me was an important conviction given the possibility that things go wrong!).

A week later I was to tell the student body that I was intending to resign, and I was feeling odd and behaving oddly. The suspects would say that I always behave oddly – what I mean is that I was responding in illogical ways to things that happened or to things that people said, the way you do (or I do) when you are under stress or worried. I had to drive up the motorway to speak at a meeting, and once again this gave me the opportunity for a long conversation with God in which I could work out what was going on. I realized that four feelings were finding indirect expression in my odd behaviour. I felt a failure for not being able to be the kind of principal the college needed (particularly given the fact that this was not the ideal time for a change of principal). I felt guilty for causing Ann to move when she would rather stay. I felt an anticipatory bereavement at the loss of people I love and who love me. And I was afraid of not finding others and of being alone. Being able to identify and name these feelings solved much of the problem, not least because I could argue with myself about them in the way Psalms 42–43 urge. You cannot argue until you have named. At the same time they remained the areas for which I had to trust God as the move drew near.

Although the telephone call from Fuller played a key part in my deciding to resign, I could not assume that there was any certainty that we would go there, and I really had dissociated the two questions. Fuller were in parallel conversations with two or three other people about the post that they wanted to fill. I did not know how the American medical insurance system worked and was not sure whether it would be financially feasible for us to abandon the arms of the British National Health Service and the social services. Neither Fuller nor we could know if we were meant for each other until we had met properly. So I needed to treat a move there as one possibility; it was no foregone conclusion. I began to read the 'Situations Vacant' columns in the church press.

When I resigned without knowing what I would do instead, I met reactions I was not prepared for. The college seemed almost hurt, as well as stunned and threatened. It was partly because almost by definition the students at a college are mostly people who like it the way it is, and they have an exaggerated idea of how far the principal decides the way it is. Admittedly I may underestimate how far that is so, not in the making of formal decisions where I may throw my weight about although in the end have only one vote, but in the setting of a style. And I remember that when I was being interviewed for the principalship I said I saw the post in terms of a guardianship of the college's relationship with God or of its spirituality, and if a person who has sought to focus on that goes, then that makes a difference. But perhaps a wife's leaving her husband for someone else is easier for him to understand than her leaving him because she simply wants a new start.

Some senior clergy seemed threatened: as a bishop said to me, 'In the Church of England you just do not resign one job until you have got the next,' and referred to Abraham's going out not knowing whither he went. Indeed, one of my colleagues had done that a year previously, resigning his post because he thought the time had come and because he thought he was about to be offered another; it gave me pause for thought that his possibility then fell through, though something else fine then emerged. 'Are you really jumping off the cliff without a safety net?' my vicar asked: to which the answer was, 'Well, we could go and live with my mother and I could become a freelance theologian' (I had not asked my mother, though when I mentioned the possibility, she did start mentally reorganizing her house). Or I might be able to become a part-time vicar and freelance theologian, and that might even enable me to continue to be a part-time Old Testament lecturer in some theological college that might need one.

Because there were such safety nets, I did not feel that a very high degree of trust was required, and did not feel as Abrahamic as I came to feel later when we knew where we were going. In the event several job possibilities arose, but the potential obstacles to going to Fuller looked as if they were melting away. A week before the visit I was invited to go for an interview for one of these other posts but I was clear that I was too committed to considering Fuller, so I declined the offer.

Soon there followed our college Quiet Day, when we have a guest speaker who gives two or three talks and there is space in the rest of the day for people to do dealings with God. I normally go to the talks but I confess that I usually let the rest pass me by, but this time it seemed appropriate not to do so. The leader encouraged us to write a letter to God, and this is what I wrote.

I like the idea of writing to you, Father – it fulfils the function of getting it out of my head, but doing it in conversation with you, and you can comment.

I am excited about the possibility of going to Fuller. You know that last Tuesday we had that lovely evening with three people from Fuller who enabled us to have a much clearer picture of what it would be like, and that on Friday I had that amazing e-mail from the Dean giving me encouraging responses to all my questions. It looks as if health care and housing and carers for Ann will not be a problem, and the job description places such an emphasis on research and writing. And I remembered that when I was articulating what I thought you were giving me permission for, in saying it was OK to leave here, I was instinctively putting it in terms of being free to be a 'writer, priest/pastor and teacher', and I thought the order must be wrong – an institution would be concerned if it thought I was mainly interested in writing. But this does not seem to be so!

The instinct to put 'priest/pastor' second is interesting, and I commit myself to that order if the job does come off. Maybe that will help with the loneliness question which is now the chief thing I am a bit anxious about. I am visualizing it as a bit like North Park [a seminary in Chicago which I had visited a little while before], with the seminary occupying the kind of space in Pasadena that North Park did there, near restaurants and shops interwoven. It will be really nice if we can find a house within a few minutes of that (like the ones in North Park) so that I can push Ann there. I think you are encouraging me to hope.

The e-mail made me feel a bit as if it was not only too good to be true, but too good to be right. I also remembered a sense that you were saying that enough was enough, that I had worked hard over the past decade with Ann and with college, and that you wanted me now to have an easier time and do what I wanted.

Although I had thus become clear that the order 'writer, pastor, teacher' was significant, at the time I was not at all clear how being a pastor would work out. Once again the answer was obvious once I had seen it. I was involved in all three of these activities at St John's (my only problem was that 'manager' was a prominent extra role, though also one which interacted with pastoring and with teaching). They are not three separate callings; they interweave. Writing is (at least sometimes) an expression of pastoring and a by-product of pastoring. Writing feeds teaching and is fed by it. Teaching feeds pastoring and is fed by it. The nature of British seminary life has always encouraged that interweaving. What God was commissioning was that I should become even more systematically one who makes the study of scripture in the classroom something which feeds life with God, and encourages students to treat me as a pastor. Some seminaries can be victims of a split between mind and relationship with God, and it was possible that I had instincts and experience which could encourage these two to be brought together more, as I knew Fuller wanted them to be.

The letter we were invited to write also involved giving to God people (whom I was concerned about, whom we will miss), situations (such as the college's future), weaknesses and temptations (such as needs I was aware of, and the possibility that we would either have not enough money, or too much), and hopes (that the post at Fuller would work out, that there would be happiness in the future for me and for Ann). I had not had the faith to ask God to make Ann happy to go to America, but before we went for our visit she was talking as if she wanted to – or was at least saying it was exciting even if she would really prefer to stay here. Her order of preference of places to live was:

Premier League: Nottingham
First Division: California, Texas, Cambridge, London, Cape Town.
Second Division: Sheffield, Scotland, Birmingham, Coventry, Melbourne, Chicago.

We flew to Los Angeles on Easter Tuesday, April 1, the day the fare went down from £434 to £299. During our first night, after a couple of hours' sleep, I was wide awake at 1.00 a.m. (it was 9.00 a.m. by my body-clock). I got up and started to read the tourist information on Los Angeles which the seminary had kindly left for us, and found myself instantly disenchanted with the prospect of living near Hollywood, Beverly Hills, and Long Beach. Glamour became tackiness; I did not want to come here. (I eventually realized that Pasadena itself is a self-contained community with its own shops, cinemas, theatres, and music, so that if we want to keep out of LA, we can do so.) I wondered what we were doing there at all and how we could get out of coming.

Yet what emerged over the next few days was that the job there was right for me and that the place was one where God had been ahead checking out for us. If there was somewhere where I could be a writer, pastor, and teacher, this was it. I had feared that the theological atmosphere would be less congenial than that at St John's, but I felt very much at home. The people were lovely, even if I allowed for the fact that (as someone put it) Americans are better at being friendly than at being friends.

I could see some of them 'falling in love with Ann', as people do, as I think of it.

On the Friday we were to be taken around some possible houses by the 'realtor' (estate agent) whom I mentioned in Chapter 12. She took us to three or four single-storey houses, which was what I had said we wanted, but my heart sank as I entered each one. I could not see us in any of them. They had tricky doorways and turns that would be difficult for Ann and the wheelchair to negotiate, and they looked literally and metaphorically 'high-maintenance': they needed work on house and garden and/or would need it on an ongoing basis, work that I lack the time or the instinct to do.

Then she took us to an apartment in a three-storey block (a 'condo' or 'condominium' because you are sharing ownership of the block). I do not know why she did that, because we had said we wanted a house. Even as we walked through the lobby with its sitting area, cool and open to the sky, I felt at home and could see us there. It was easy to push the wheelchair round the ground-floor open-plan apartment. There was a study area which was semi-separate from the lounge, a version of the way we had arranged things at our home in Nottingham so that I can be with Ann but be working (fingers in ears when interesting television coincides with something I need to think hard about).

In due course we walked into the bathroom and there was a walk-in shower of the kind we had installed in our home in Nottingham. I half-saw the hand of God pointing, and half-heard God saying, 'Do you see?': which I took to mean, 'I've been here before, I knew this was here, it's for you.' I say 'half-saw' and 'half-heard' because at the time it seemed naive and too risky even to think that that might be what was going on, but as weeks passed I gained confidence in believing that this was for us. It seemed significant that the vendor was an Anglican (a rarer thing in the USA than in Britain) who was glad to be selling to someone in Christian ministry, and was willing to drop the price by $15,000. It seemed significant that the condo stayed on the market for the period of weeks until I was offered a job and accepted it; subsequently another sold at a higher price within five days.

Ann coped well with the journey, and if anything moved a little easier than she had been doing in Britain. This confirmed the possibility that the climate would be good for her. A few months previously when Fuller had invited me to discuss the possibility of a post, I had said that Ann could hardly come to somewhere hot. The Dean, whose sister-in-law has multiple sclerosis, pointed out that California has a desert climate – sunny and hot but with low humidity. We already knew that suited Ann. We have been for a number of holidays in the Alps because there you get warm sun but low humidity. On the first occasion there, when Ann could get about with just a walking stick, she was upset when we got home because she could walk in the Alps and not back in Nottingham.

After we returned to Britain, the seminary had to go through the rest of its procedures, which included considering the other possible candidates. We also had to do some thinking. Although the salary would be much higher, so would our expenses, and I needed to check that we could make the finances work. I also needed to think about other aspects of care for Ann and to say things to Fuller about the kind of provision she would need.

One Wednesday, nearly three weeks after our return, we had a time of seeking God in college chapel, and God told one of our students, 'Tell John: "Judges 18:6" '. 'I don't know what it says,' she replied, 'and I haven't got a Bible.' (Never go to church without a Bible!) 'Never mind,' said God, 'just tell him: "Judges 18.6".' Later in the corridor she pressed into my hand a scrap of paper bearing this reference and told me what had happened. 'Judges 18? That's the story of the Levite's concubine being cut into twelve pieces, isn't it?' I said. 'I hope not,' she replied (actually that is Judges 19, though as a whole Judges 18 is fairly tough stuff, too). We both went home to look it up. In the NIV it reads: 'Go in peace. Your journey has the LORD's approval.' The NRSV has: 'Go in peace. The mission you are on is under the eye of the LORD.' I checked the Hebrew, which says more literally: 'Go in peace. The road on which you are going is before Yahweh.' It reminds me now of that sense that God had checked out 111 South Orange Grove ahead of us. The word for 'before' is a rare one. The dictionary explains that in contexts such as this it means 'under Yahweh's eye and favourable regard'. It is worth learning Hebrew.

It was the next day that I received an e-mail offering me the job at Fuller and making a commitment with regard to Ann that did not leave me without risk but reduced that risk to something I ought to be prepared to accept. It seemed a 'defining moment', as one of my colleagues put it, though I felt quite cold about it. I gained no pleasure or sense of excitement such as I had felt in the spring term about the prospect. But I could not get out of the sense of being carried on a conveyer-belt – not merely by Fuller but by events as a whole, and by God. It was odd that I felt so cold, though I did not mind. Perhaps there was too much to feel.

I printed out the message, wandered about with it that day, and slept on it, though I knew there was only one response I could make. In the meantime, that evening I went to pray with three of the suspects, and one prayed not for pleasure but for joy. Next day after chapel I went to the computer again and typed a short note of acceptance. As I paused before I pressed the 'Send' key, intending perhaps to think and pray one more time, a colleague came in to ask me about something. We had a brief conversation and I turned back to the keyboard. I found that actually I had pressed the 'Send' key without noticing (or someone had). It was too late for further thoughts. That somehow seemed right and typical. All through this had been something that God and other people were in charge of. That was so even at the point of saying 'Yes'.

The same afternoon we had a corporate time of prayer in college, and as we began in worship I was overwhelmed with a joy in praising God. On Friday evening it was the college revue, which we enjoyed, and I sang 'Route 66', the song popularized in Britain by the Rolling Stones, about the road from Chicago to Los Angeles via Pasadena; our house is a few blocks off it. I danced a bit but realized that my heart was not really in it and wandered off homewards.

The set readings and prayers that Sunday were just for me. We prayed to God who can bring order to our unruly wills and passions. We heard God promising to turn desolation into beauty. We heard God knocking at the door seeking to be let in. We heard God asking, 'Do you love me more than these?' (e.g. these books).

Over the next few weeks, I had to concentrate too much on college matters to worry much about the future. There were funny things that happened. For a while it seemed that we were caught in a kind of Catch 22. Our mortgage broker wanted us to sign documents at the US embassy in London during June. Our immigration attorney wanted us go nowhere near the embassy about our loan before we had a visa. By the time we had a visa it would be too late for the loan. Or we could find ourselves losing both loan and visa. . . . In due course these two questions became unlinked and the house purchase was going through. I wired our payment to the agent. The money failed to arrive. The seminary bursar asked for reference numbers to enable them to chase the transaction. That week a landing on Mars was being orchestrated from Pasadena; the college joke was that we had unintentionally bought real estate there. By the time I had the reference numbers, it was Independence Day and everyone had gone on holiday for a long weekend. But after the weekend the money reappeared from cyberspace, the sale went through, and we were part-owners of a condominium in California. I could imagine how nice it would be to be able to push Ann in the wheelchair to the city to restaurants, cinemas and shops (we could go nowhere by wheel-chair-push in Nottingham). I could imagine how nice it might be to picnic by the condo's pool.

Of course for some reason we might not get visas; we would be owning a property in the USA but unable to enter the country to earn the money to pay for it. Indeed, the embassy initially refused our visa application; Ann's photograph was too small. Fortunately in due course it transpired that this was their biggest problem with us, and we had the visas. Then I really believed we were going.

From time to time I fretted about Ann. We had warm spring weather in April and our garden looked lovely; I could not imagine her enjoying looking out on our patio in Pasadena in the same way. I had to give that to God, believing the signs of God's involvement. From time to time I was overwhelmed by the stress of all the questions involved in the move. It was from then on that I was to have that recurrent feeling that I had never been so pushed out in faith, having to trust in demanding circumstances. What if we did not find the companions we needed to look after Ann? What might issue from the fact that we did not really know how the medical system works in the USA and what it will deliver? What if I am unable to cope physically? What if I am unable to cope emotionally? One Sunday I told our churchwarden that the thing that scared me most was loneliness. She said one had to remember that the fact that you were not with people did not mean that they had stopped loving you; I have to remember that. But more profoundly I have to remember that God has directed us there, God had been there before and looked, and that every week God gives us an encouragement, a sign of love, provision, and divine sense of humour.

By then the stakes had been raised. During the summer term Ann had been getting less mobile and in late June had a relapse of her illness. She could no longer stand at all and her catheter system no longer worked. She was admitted to her rehabilitation centre for four weeks and came out less mobile than she was when she went in. This markedly changed the nature of the task of caring for her. I learned to use a 'hoist' and discovered that the nicer American term is patient-lift, but the medics were uncertain about how to handle the catheter problem. Apart from that being unpleasant for Ann and tricky if we are out (let alone on an aircraft for eleven hours), it threatens skin problems. So how would we cope here, and how cope there? Neither Fuller nor I have a bottomless purse to cover possible nursing costs. And all this heightens the pressure of the fact that we are moving away from the people who love us and whom we love. I have realized that half-an-hour's conversation with one of those people is part of what keeps me going: what will replace it?

So what does trust mean? What can I trust God for? There had been all those signs that God was taking us from the UK to the USA, and in a dream I could imagine that everything would be wonderful. We would get the companions. We would get the

198

To The Usual Suspects

health care. Ann's catheter system would work, or we would find some other arrangement. I would be able to walk her into the town for a film or ice cream or shopping. We would attract squirrels and birds onto our patio. But I was making the mistake of trying to imagine a neat future by analogy with the present, the way you have to when you think of heaven. It is a mistake, but it is all you can do. I had to remind myself that in this new situation, things working out well and in a way that makes Ann happy will be different and is by definition unimaginable. All I could do is imagine re-creating what works here; 'working well' there will probably be quite different.

There was a much tougher fact that I had to remind myself of. There were all those signs that God was taking us from the UK to the USA, yet I was hesitant to believe that God was promising us a rose garden, that they implied that everything was bound to be well. Somehow things do not necessarily work out that way. After all, we sought to be sure that our marrying in the first place was God's will, but this has not stopped its being tough. Lots of people who seek God's will regarding who they marry end up divorced.

So what is one entitled to expect? What does God's faithfulness consist in? I suppose that my own experience has been that each extra bit of pressure has been but the harbinger of another one. God treats me rather the way a trainer treats a weightlifter. The satisfaction you get is not that of now being able to give up lifting weights. Succeeding at one weight simply qualifies you to try the next. When the possibility of going to Pasadena first arose, it felt like a gift, like the trainer's permission to rest. By the time we were about to leave, it felt more like the context in which to lift some more weights. The faithfulness of God consists in not requiring you to lift what will break your back; the promise is that God does not let us be tested beyond our strength. That is my bottom-line trust. I trust that in personal ways things will not be overwhelming, that I will be able to carry the inner burden, and that in financial ways things will not be overwhelming.

One night when I had been away for the day, on getting back to Nottingham I went to see Ann in the rehabilitation centre in the late evening. She was in bed, and she greeted me with a surprised smile. I had written on her message board that I would be there late and had asked the nurses to remind her; perhaps they had done so and she had forgotten. She had had no visitors. I had asked God to send someone, but there had apparently been no one (though perhaps someone had been, and Ann had forgotten). Her contentedness seemed to make that not matter. On my way out a nurse stopped me to ask one or two things and then talked about how wonderful it was that we were going to America and how wonderful Ann was. She told me how much they had been laughing in the afternoon as they had been getting her to bed with the hoist, and how wonderful her sense of humour was. I came home crying but content, as I often am, feeling that for me and for Ann God had not done what I asked, but had ministered to me and to her in ways that made that OK.

A fortnight later Ann came home. For twenty-four hours it seemed that looking after her was all there was time to do. I got up with some sense of hopelessness the next day, when she had been home for thirty-six hours. In the post I found a 'bon voyage' card from a former student. It was embroidered on the front with a boat bearing the stars and stripes and our initials, and superimposed on this was the cross. Inside it talked about what college had meant to this person and the blessings that had come through Ann's illness. The previous day I had been reading 2 Corinthians 4 because I had to preach on it a week or two later: 'death is at work in us, but life in you'. That has been Ann's story. And mine, in a way (though in mine I can see life at work as well; I have to trust God to work that out for Ann).

That evening one of my dreads happened. Ann needed to go to the toilet in the evening when I was on my own. I was not at all sure how on earth we could manage this, but it was OK.

And that night I had a dream. Near our home there is a six-lane road with a complicated junction to take you towards where we live. At the time the road was being repaired and only four of six lanes were open. As you drove along you switched from one lane to another, sometimes with holes and barriers on one side, sometimes on the other. In my dream the junction itself was under reconstruction and I was travelling through it on a bus. There was only the narrowest of carriageways through the roadworks and the surface was not tarred. Indeed, the carriageway was not actually wide enough for the bus, and it crumbled down on either side into deep gulfs. It was like a nightmare version of French, or even more of Israeli, roadworks. But the bus made its way briskly and confidently through the junction and on towards our home. I took that as God's promise regarding the journey we were about to undertake. Later I discovered that when God promises to make the way of the righteous smooth, in Isaiah 29, the word for 'way' is the word for a cart-track, and cart-tracks are pretty uneven, like Israeli roadworks.

There came a time when every day there seemed to be another goodbye, that time when every time we said goodbye they took a little part of us and we died a little. These were people who were themselves grieved (even angry!) that we were going. With all of them there were words or just gestures which made it clear that we were loved and would be missed. And because I am still rather dazed by the idea of being loved, that has the more of an impact. On our farewell Sunday at our church one of our churchwardens gave us a card with the promise 'God is not a deceiver that he should offer to support us and then when we lean upon him should slip away from us'. And on the congregational farewell card our vicar copied an inscription in Welsh which he had seen in St David's Cathedral in Wales: 'Bydd gytiawn ac nad ofna'. Although he is Welsh, he claimed not to understand it – or rather because he is Welsh, he claimed it was untranslatable – but he eventually agreed that it meant something like 'Be whole without fear'. We have to trust and be that.

I wrote all that before we left but have recast it in the past tense as we have now been in Pasadena for a few months. I felt before we left that God's own trustworthiness was on the line, and that because God had put it there.

If things went wrong, God would be in more of a mess than I would. But over the past twenty weeks God has proved that that trustworthiness is real. Indeed, I have to say that the way that God has proved trustworthy over the twenty weeks since we came here has gone far beyond my dreams. We have had lots of little crises but none that God has not taken us through to the other side of and then smiled lovingly and said, 'You see, it turned out OK, didn't it?' I have felt that being here as just a professor is an even more wonderful relief from the stress of being in charge than I imagined. Ann has moved from 'I don't want to go' to 'It's better here than I expected' to 'I like America more than England', and that is something I would not have dared pray for.

Half-way through the first term, one Tuesday in a time of informal worship, someone prayed that God would guard what God had written on our hearts, and next morning I wrote down some of those things to God, those things that God had written on my heart, again almost like a letter. Some of what I wrote then, and have added since, is:

- You love me like a protector with warmth and affection and steel.
- This is the right place for me and it will be a place of refreshment.
- I am to give myself and will then find myself.
- You have given me the vocation of living with Ann's illness, and I accept it.
- You want me to prove that living with loss isn't incompatible with living with joy, and I accept that too, enthusiastically.

At the beginning of our second term I was asked to give a testimony in chapel, and I told people something of this story. At the end of the service a student came up to me and told me how in the worship part he had been given a picture of a man standing washing dishes, looking out over a garden, and of God saying, 'I have heard you.' As I spoke he knew the picture was for me. As we wept on each other's shoulders, I knew that this was not me here in Pasadena (where I wash dishes facing a wall!) but me in Nottingham where I indeed washed dishes facing the garden with its fruit trees and birds and squirrels which Ann and I both loved. I knew that the picture was true, though only as I write do I realize its significance. I believed then that God was listening and that God would make things work out, but by the nature of the case this had to be faith not sight. Now it was sight, and God was once again saying (in love, not in rebuke), 'Do you see? I was listening, wasn't I?' I shall probably realize something else tomorrow, but I have to post this disk . . .

Of course I am still working to trust God for the longer-term issues. Trusting does not have an end – even in heaven: see 1 Corinthians 13.13? Some of the suspects would say it is just like me to end with a question mark, so I am glad I have been able to do it.

157 - Healing and repentance
174 - Headship + submission.